DAVID WILLIAMSON's first full-length play, *The Coming of Stork*, premiered at the La Mama Theatre, Carlton, in 1970 and later became the film *Stork*, directed by Tim Burstall.

The Removalists and *Don's Party* followed in 1971, then *Jugglers Three* (1972), *What If You Died Tomorrow?* (1973), *The Department* (1975), *A Handful of Friends* (1976), *The Club* (1977) and *Travelling North* (1979). In 1972 *The Removalists* won the Australian Writers' Guild AWGIE Award for best stage play and the best script in any medium and the British production saw Williamson nominated most promising playwright by the London *Evening Standard*.

The 1980s saw his success continue with *Celluloid Heroes* (1980), *The Perfectionist* (1982), *Sons of Cain* (1985), *Emerald City* (1987) and *Top Silk* (1989); whilst the 1990s produced *Siren* (1990), *Money and Friends* (1991), *Brilliant Lies* (1993), *Sanctuary* (1994), *Dead White Males* (1995), *Heretic* (1996), *Third World Blues* (an adaptation of *Jugglers Three*) and *After the Ball* (both in 1997), and *Corporate Vibes* and *Face to Face* (both in 1999). *The Great Man* (2000), *Up for Grabs*, *A Conversation*, *Charitable Intent* (all in 2001), *Soulmates* (2002) and *Birthrights* (2003) have since followed.

Williamson is widely recognised as Australia's most successful playwright and over the last thirty years his plays have been performed throughout Australia and produced in Britain, United States, Canada and many European countries. A number of his stage works have been adapted for the screen, including *The Removalists, Don's Party, The Club, Travelling North, Emerald City, Sanctuary* and *Brilliant Lies*.

David Williamson has won the Australian Film Institute film script award for *Petersen* (1974), *Don's Party* (1976), *Gallipoli* (1981) and *Travelling North* (1987) and has won eleven Australian Writers' Guild AWGIE Awards. He lives on Queensland's Sunshine Coast with his writer wife, Kristin Williamson.

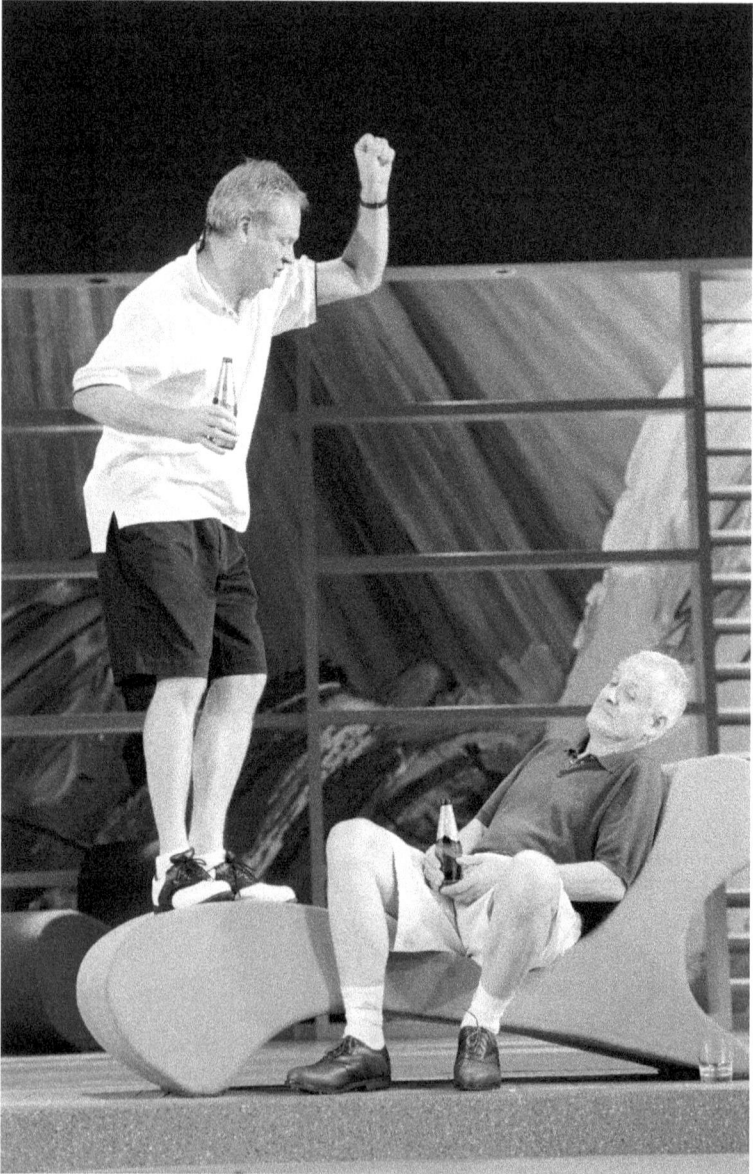

Gary Day as Jim and Tony Llewellyn-Jones as Dick in the 2004 Sydney Theatre Company production. (Photo: Tracey Schramm)

David Williamson
Amigos

Currency Press, Sydney

CURRENCY PLAYS

Amigos first published in 2004
by Currency Press Pty Ltd,
PO Box 2287, Strawberry Hills, NSW, 2012, Australia
enquiries@currency.com.au
www.currency.com.au

NATIONAL LIBRARY OF AUSTRALIA CIP DATA
Williamson, David, 1942–.
Amigos.
ISBN 0 86819 746 7.
I. Title. (Series: Currency plays).
A822.3

Set by Dean Nottle
Cover design by Kate Florance
Front cover shows Gary Day as Jim and Tony Llewellyn-Jones as Dick in the
2004 Sydney Theatre Company production. (Photo: Tracey Schramm)

Contents

Currency Press acknowledges the Traditional Owners of the
Country on which we live and work. We pay our respects to all
Aboriginal and Torres Strait Islander Elders, past and present.

Wendy Hughes as Hilary and Garry McDonald as Stephen in the 2004 Sydney Theatre Company production. (Photo: Tracey Schramm)

The Costs of Masculinity:
Placing Men's Pain in the Context of Male Power

A Crisis in Masculinity?

If the popular media is to be believed, men and boys are having a really tough time lately. We are bombarded in the media on an almost daily basis with evidence of how badly off males are—in their health status, in their emotional lives, and in their educational achievements. Even politicians are talking about a 'crisis of masculinity'. A lot of seemingly factual information is presented, but rarely is the question asked—what does it all mean? In the absence of any genuine attempt at understanding, the suspicion is left that it is somehow 'women's fault', that girls have gained at boys' expense, and what we need is a reassertion of traditional masculine values. Naturally enough, this often arouses impatience, frustration or outright hostility from those groups which experience the real consequences of men's power—after all, there is nothing quite so off-putting as listening to someone moan about how hard it is to be privileged!

However, we cannot avoid the fact that the subjective experience of personal suffering is very real to many men. The ways in which men make sense of this pain will influence their relationships with women, with their families, and impact on the choices they make in their lives. For this reason, I believe that the project of representing and interpreting this pain has considerable political and cultural importance. It is in this context that David Williamson's *Amigos* is particularly welcome. It is a powerful presentation of the emotional costs of masculine culture, of the corrosive effects of the pursuit of success above all else, and of the ultimate hollowness of some men's claims to friendship. While this may seem a particularly bleak vision, I believe that it is an accurate portrayal of important aspects of dominant male culture in Australia today.

I hope that this play will provide a focus for conversations about the real costs of masculinity; for these conversations are very badly needed in a society that is all too dominated by the hyper-masculinity of the war against terror, bear pit politics, shock jocks and elite male sports. However, if such conversations are to take place in a constructive way, they will need to be informed by an understanding of how masculine culture operates and reproduces itself. This introduction is my contribution to these hoped for conversations.

POWER

Numerous western scholars have identified the pursuit of power for its own sake, as the supreme value of patriarchal culture,[1] and it is certainly a regular theme among philosophers. According to Nietzsche 'joy is only a symptom of the feeling of attained power. The essence of joy is a plus-feeling of power.'[2] Hegel attributes the emergence of human consciousness itself to the 'fear of annihilation by other men. To know yourself as a man is to know that other men may enslave and destroy you.'[3]

For men, two things seem to go inextricably together—the desire for power and the fear of failure. No other alternative seems to exist. The authors of one study in Britain concluded that 'to be a loser is to suffer a terrible fate. In the course of therapy with men, we find that no matter how great their success, they are haunted by the spectre of failure. Indeed it is our impression that men are driven much more by fear of failure than by the desire to succeed.'[4]

'To be a man it is not enough simply to be: A man must do, display, prove, in order to establish unchallenged manhood'.[5] All of the major signifiers of manhood are continually under threat or intrinsically transitory—money, political power, physical strength, sexual performance. Lynne Segal notes that men's oppressiveness comes from their 'wretched fear of not being male-enough'.[6] 'Making a man out of a boy' means teaching him that the human sacrifices of the power struggle are essential to the process of becoming a man. Institutions that make men out of boys have historically involved brutalisation, physical and emotional abuse, emphasis on hardness and strength, contempt for sensitivity, delicacy and emotional intimacy. Not all boys experience such treatment, but they are all aware of its existence. Marilyn French notes that 'no boy escapes the knowledge of the severities of "manliness" in our society, and those who feel they have not achieved it live with lingering self-doubt, self-diminishment'.[7]

This masculine obsession with power and control is brilliantly embodied by Jim in *Amigos*. He revels in being the hawk, lulling his victim into a false sense of security and then stooping in for the kill. As Dick says: 'The moment he loves best is when the mouse looks at him and realises he's about to die'. Jim is incapable of seeing life in terms other than that of winners and losers. He even classifies his allegedly closest friends in this way, discarding those who don't make the grade.

ATTITUDES TOWARDS WOMEN

Masculinity is often most clearly defined in terms of what it is not— what it is afraid of being—and what men most definitely are not is women. Men are men because they don't cry, don't feel, don't need, and contempt for women is a deeply ingrained characteristic of our culture. The contempt for women implicit in masculinity is demonstrated in all sorts of ways. Where men are ridiculed in cartoons and on television, it is usually because they are under the control of women. To diminish a man it is only necessary to depict him doing the dishes, sewing, or wearing an apron, and most of the worst forms of ridicule and abuse applied to men involve comparison with women. 'Mummy's boy' is an insult that most boys will do almost anything to avoid, and sports coaches routinely tell boys that they are playing 'like girls' to urge them on to greater efforts.[8]

This need to define themselves against women fuels a basic masculine inner conflict. This begins with the requirement that boys separate themselves from their mothers, who have generally been the source of almost all the love and security in the boys' lives.[9] The breaking of this emotional connection between boys and their mothers produces a deeply dehumanising split which is maintained by dividing men amongst themselves as well as against women. Women are defined as inferior, and men are defined as competitors, rather than as allies. A 'real man' stands alone—apart from women and from other men. He is independent and self-sufficient. Above all, he copes without complaint.

Because of this, men are generally not well equipped to deal with the emotional requirements of an adult relationship. Dominant masculine beliefs get in the way of men being able to experience their sexuality as a source of pleasure, that can be easily and openly shared in a context of equity and mutuality. In particular, the focus on power and competition, and the need to be in control, sets up barriers that are not easy to drop. Masculinity is not simply a belief system, that men experience 'in their heads'. It is part of the construction of their bodies and bodily responses. Masculinity is about hardness and conflict, and the need to be constantly on guard—none of which is conducive to the easy enjoyment of self and other.

The idea that some level of domination is essential to male sexual excitement is quite common in our society. Maslow, for example, asserted that 'normal sexual happiness can only occur in our society when the male plays the dominant role'.[10] This is supported by the cultural insistence that men should be older, taller, wealthier, more educated, more intelligent and with higher social status than their female partners. It is supported by the erotic idealisation of young women, and many men's preference for them as sexual partners.[11]

Sexual relationships between men and women are particularly problematic because it is in this context that men often experience women as most powerful. According to Lynne Segal:

> It seems likely that men are least sure of their power over women, and most fearful of women's self-sufficiency and autonomy, precisely in their sexual encounters with them.[12]

> For many men, it is precisely through sex that they experience their greatest uncertainties, dependence and deference in relation to women—in stark contrast, quite often, to their experience of authority and independence in the public world.[13]

One of the attractions of paid sex for men is that it provides an opportunity to escape conventional, male heterosexual roles, and to do things that they could never allow themselves to do with their actual partner.[14] In a paid sex encounter, men know that they can simply walk away afterwards, and the woman has no more claim on them. In their own relationships, however, men's sense of women's power makes emotional vulnerability and the enjoyment of passivity, for example, a much more threatening proposition.

This complexity is wonderfully portrayed through the couple relationships in *Amigos*. Jim, for example, is completely incapable of entering into an equal relationship. He says of his lover, Sophie:

We were the perfect team. I'd do the cut and thrust and she'd do the backup. And stroke my ego... We all need a cheer squad, me more than most. But marry your cheer leader and she's suddenly on an equal footing and it's hell... Sweet compliant PA suddenly becomes Sophie ball buster.

In some ways, Jim's and Dick's relationships represent the alternatives many men believe they are faced with—Jim has sex but no friendship with Sophie, and Dick has friendship but no sex with Hilary. Each is incapable of entering fully into a relationship with his partner, because they are too afraid of the lack of control that would involve. Instead, Jim chooses a partner he continually refers to as a 'kid', and Dick resorts to paid sex to fulfil his fantasies.

TURNING BOYS INTO MEN

The process of turning boys into men incapable of open, equal relationships is enforced largely by other men. Fathers brutalise sons, in the interest of toughening them up to survive in a harsh world. Groups of boys turn on those who are different, and instil a fervent desire not to stand out from the crowd. Team sports and military service continue to be widely valued as ways of turning boys into men. They provide the essential ingredients of violent competition, the willingness to inflict pain on others in order to win, and obedience to the 'captain'. They are both about toughening men so that they learn to ignore pain and emotions, and both use being 'like a girl' as the ultimately humiliating reprimand.

This toughening plays a direct social function. Peter Lewis, discussing his time in the army argues:

Under that regime women stood for emotions and feelings that might, unless they were outlawed, impede discipline. In the end, a trigger had to be pulled, a button pressed and it took 'men' to do it because only men were capable of surrendering all compassion.[15]

Male camaraderie or 'mateship' is founded on sharing the rituals of masculine identity. The exclusion of women is an integral aspect, and many of these rituals turn out to be destructive or oppressive. Binge drinking, gambling and violent sports are obvious examples. Men become close through the experience of battle, through conquering the wilderness, hunting, breaking the law and even through the ritual of pack rape.[16] This kind of male friendship, however, is extremely fragile. If unspoken limits are transgressed or rules broken, then the full fury of male condemnation rapidly descends upon the head of the guilty party. The end result is a deep seated fear of difference.

The fragility of male friendship is one of the most powerful themes emerging from *Amigos*. With no sense of the contradictions involved, Jim can declare:

> *When the four of us got up on that dais and they put the medals around our necks, and the tears were flowing—that's lifetime bond territory. Unbreakable.*

and, yet still say of Stephen:

> *He was a weird recluse then, and he's even weirder now. He was never a fucking friend. He was just the fourth rower we needed to win gold. And he wasn't even good enough to do that. Can we stop all this sentimental bullshit!*

For Jim, power and success have become the only lens through which the world is viewed. Friendship simply cannot stand in the way of this imperative, and even Jim's 'closest friend' Dick, is subjected to blackmail and bribery in the pursuit of his desired goals. Anyone who makes choices outside of the dominant masculine frame of reference— whether it is his ex-wife's 'alternative lifestyle' or Stephen's writing— is simply ridiculed and dismissed.

Probably the most crucial way of dividing men amongst themselves and punishing difference is through the taboo against homosexuality. Homophobia is a powerful weapon for preventing challenge to masculine ways of being. Theorists of masculinity have shown how:

> *the homosexual—heterosexual dichotomy acts as a central symbol in all rankings of masculinity. Any kind of power-lessness, or refusal to compete, among men readily becomes involved with the imagery of homosexuality.*[17]

Most men know full well the fear of being labelled a 'poofter' at any sign of difference, particularly in the expression of affection or weakness. Again, David Williamson manages to weave this thread into *Amigos* very effectively. Jim expresses classic homophobia in his contempt and disgust for Roger. He clearly equates homosexuality with weakness, blaming the relationship between Roger and Dick for the team's failure to win gold.

MEN AND INSTITUTIONS

One of the central paradoxes of masculinity is that while men, as a group, clearly hold the reins of power, the majority of men experience themselves as powerless.[18] Most men, if they are lucky enough to have a job, work in some sort of institution, which is hierarchically structured and which generally allows them little sense of personal agency. According to Marilyn French, 'institutions are created to centralise, harness and manifest power over others'.[19] They appeal to individuals by promising personal power—but these promises are largely illusory. The power is lodged in the institution, not in any particular person.

All of the institutions within which men lead their lives are implicitly or explicitly hierarchical. From the family, with the father as the (at least nominal) head, through schools and sporting teams, the church, business, industry, trade unions, politics, law, crime, prisons, hospitals, medicine—they all encourage striving for success, which may involve stepping on the shoulders of one's friends and associates. The struggle and the structure tend to become all absorbing, and men are encouraged to regard all other parts of life as secondary.[20] The pursuit of power and control denies men love and sensuality, and leaves only desire and the excitement of conquest. Men are generally distant from their children and partners, and their working lives are dominated by competition and mistrust. The higher men go on the ladder of success, the harder it is for them to trust other men and to make real friendships.[21]

In *Amigos,* the extreme of this situation is brilliantly portrayed in Jim's and Dick's friendship. Jim acknowledges that he has 'Alliances, Dick. Strategic alliances. Not friends.', but at the same time he claims Dick as his one real friend. However, he feels humiliated by the fact that Dick has received greater public recognition than he has, and sets out to blackmail and bribe him in order to rectify the situation. Dick, on the other hand, revels in his opportunity to turn the tables on his otherwise more powerful friend:

> *He's always been the hare and I've been the tortoise, but the tortoise plodded on and worked quietly and hard and added*

*years to the lives of men who count. And I got an AC. And
I'll have the new heart wing of a great Australian hospital
named after me in a year's time, so he can just bloody well
suffer!*

As Hilary says, 'If this is your oldest friend I'd hate to hear you talking
about an enemy'. Stephen is exactly right when he replies, 'Things are
complicated with men'.

Men's working lives, particularly in the corporate world, are a
permanent battlefield, with countless casualties, whose failure only
serves to increase the prestige of those who succeed. The myth is
maintained that everyone can be a winner if only he tries hard enough,
and every man who fails believes it is because he is not good enough,
rather than because the system is inherently wrong. Clearly, not every
man is a winner, and many men's lives are ruled, not so much by an
active desire for power and success, but by the inner knowledge of
having failed as a man, and the determination not to be discovered.

This is even the case with men, such as Jim, who seem to have been
the most successful. Jim's desire to receive the 'AC' and his sense of
humiliation at not getting it, demonstrate the fragility of his professed
success and self-sufficiency. However much he may see himself as the
'hawk' and despise all those around him, he is still ultimately dependent
on them for the recognition he craves. The robust individualism of
dominant masculinity is ultimately revealed as a façade, behind which
lurk all sorts of fears and insecurities.

EMOTION

This brings us to the question of emotion. Thanks to pop psychology it
is now almost a truism that men lean heavily towards emotional
illiteracy. Talk shows and women's magazines bemoan the fact that
men are not allowed to express their vulnerable and nurturing emotions,
and are consequently psychologically and socially deformed. While
there is considerable truth in this picture, it leaves out a crucial part of
the whole. In particular, there seems to be little awareness of the gendered
power structures within which emotions are constructed and expressed.

It is certainly true that the public display by men of emotions, other
than anger, is generally judged very negatively in our culture. The
process of turning boys into men has, historically, been one of systematic

abuse, both physical and emotional, designed to teach boys not to show most emotions, except in certain ritually prescribed circumstances. Boys are taught to fear intimacy and self-revelation, as the consequences are generally pain and humiliation at the hands of other boys, and to hate whatever causes them to experience fear.[22]

The consequences of this process are wonderfully drawn out in *Amigos*, particularly through the character of Stephen. It takes the painful death of his son Daniel to make him realise how much they both need each other's love. Speaking to Sophie, Stephen says:

> *A couple of weeks before he died Daniel looked at me and said, 'Dad, let it out. If you're feeling something, tell me.' The tears started rolling out of my eyes, but I still couldn't let it out. He got angry and said, 'For fuck's sake, Dad, say it. Whatever it is, say it. What are you feeling?'. I said, 'I'm feeling that I love you, but I don't have a clue how to say it.' And he said, 'You've just said it. It's taken me nearly twenty-four years to ever hear it, but you've just said it.' And we cried and hugged each other for the very first time in our lives.*

It is a tragic reality that many men never realise how much they are missing in their lives until it is too late. All too often they have to lose their children or their partners before they can admit to the harm they are causing themselves and others and begin the painful process of change. Unfortunately, many men also respond to such losses with blame and attack, rather than with a willingness to open up and look at themselves.

Stephen's character exhibits a number of other attributes that help make sense of the fact that he, alone of the male characters, is able to 'cross the line' and openly express a broad range of emotions. Only he refused to take performance enhancing drugs during the 'Amigos' Olympic career and he chose to leave a 'top job as an actuary' in order to be a creative writer. There was clearly a history to his ability to finally open up to his son, and we are left with the impression that the dominant masculine values embraced by Jim and, to a lesser extent, Dick are extraordinarily constrictive to men's fundamental humanity. Dominant masculinity subordinates everything to power and success, and in the process personal ethics, empathy, emotional openness and creativity have to be sacrificed.

However, it is crucial to recognise the function that men's 'emotional illiteracy' has in the maintenance of power structures—whether based on gender, class or race. Emotional numbness or indifference is a powerful weapon—it allows a person to inflict pain on others without being affected or swayed. Some important studies have shown how the power wielded by soldiers stems from their lack of self-reflection and empathy, while their training involves dehumanising and demonising the enemy. It is important to recognise that this is only an extreme form of general masculine training.[23]

Men, I would argue, are not simply victims of distorted emotional roles. Their pain and suffering are real, but they also hide feelings in order to withhold information which might give others power over them. Men's pain is not the cause of their abuse of power, rather, the structured abuse of power requires men to be emotionally abused and desensitised. Masculinity consists of those personality traits that are necessary for the preservation and perpetuation of an unjust and oppressive system. It creates the emotional splitting and illiteracy that then allows men to abuse others, as well as being susceptible to emotional manipulation by those in positions of power. While not all men benefit equally from the system, they do provide its shock troops and rank-and-file enforcers, as well as its generals. They provide cannon fodder for the factories, offices and unemployment lines, and without their participation and compliance the system could not continue.

ARE MEN OPPRESSED?

This, finally, brings me to the common claim that men are in danger of being left behind by contemporary social and economic change, and are therefore entitled to think of themselves as a disadvantaged, or even oppressed, group. It is clear—at least to me—that men suffer as a consequence of conforming to the values of dominant masculinity. Even those who seem to benefit most do so at enormous personal cost. To argue otherwise is to accept patriarchy's lies—that the pursuit of power, to the exclusion of all else, can lead to happiness and a sense of personal fulfilment. I don't believe it, and all the studies I have seen indicate the opposite. *Amigos* is itself a powerful presentation of this fact. But does the fact that many men are indeed having a hard time entitle them to regard themselves as disadvantaged or 'oppressed'? My answer is a definite 'No!'.

'Disadvantage' and 'oppression' should be understood as referring to relationships between groups within complex networks of social power. 'Advantage' involves the occupation of strategic points in these networks by particular groups, who then use their position of dominance to exclude, exploit and demean people who do not 'belong'. Institutions are those bodies that structure and control the crucial points in these networks of power, and there can be no doubt that the most powerful institutions in our society are still occupied, at the highest levels, almost exclusively by men.

Where women are included, it is only after demonstrating allegiance to the institution's values, and the more women there are in an institution, the lower its status in the overall hierarchical structure of society. While individual men may not possess much power, the fact of being a man does not in itself disqualify anyone from entry to our society's most powerful institutions. Individuals or groups of men may be barred on the grounds of their class or race, for example, but they are not barred on the grounds of gender. For every woman, her gender alone makes it considerably more difficult to even get through the door.

CONCLUSION

Whatever their behaviour may suggest, I am convinced that men want intimacy, trust and love in their relationships. Unfortunately, they continue acting in ways and subscribing to values that end up destroying the very things they long for. The focus on power and success results in many men becoming extraordinarily self centred, making empathy and compassion particularly difficult to access. Men continue to believe that they can compartmentalise their lives, subscribing to one set of values in public, and to another in private. Experience suggests that this is ultimately impossible, and that friendship and relationships are the eventual casualties.

At the end of *Amigos*, Jim and Dick are forced to make some major concessions to keep their relationships, yet we are not left with a sense of optimism. Jim still delights in destroying his competitors and Dick is willing to accept money in order to get his 'name up in stone'. They both admit that they can't live without their wives and that these women are indeed their only true friends. Yet they are locked into values and behaviours that are ultimately incompatible with the trust and honesty necessary in true friendship.

None of this is meant to suggest that these dilemmas are exclusively male. Fear of difference, anger, desire for power and lust for revenge are fundamental human experiences—yet this is territory that has been mainly colonised by men and staked out as their particular domain. However, moving away from this familiar territory can indeed be scary. As Stephen recognises, life is not fair. It is characterised by randomness and impermanence. No matter how close our relationships, we are all ultimately parted by death. As Stephen says:

> *Life is about connection, they chant. Connection with others. Sure. Then they die and you go crazy with grief.*

Much of dominant masculinity is a vain attempt to deny this very pain and vulnerability. However, the attempt is doomed—no one, no matter how powerful, can protect themselves against loss and ultimately death. In my opinion, we would all be far better off if men could learn to embrace this uncertainty, stop trying to be in control, and open themselves to the joys as well as the difficulties that come with honest, open and equal relationships.

---

[1] French, M. (1991) *Beyond Power: On women, men and morals*, London: Cardinal, p 354; Miles, R. (1991) *The Rites of Man: Love, sex and death in the making of the male*, London: Grafton, pp 200–5; Middleton, P. (1992) *The Inward Gaze: Masculinity and subjectivity in modern culture*, London: Routledge, p 213.

[2] Miles, p 200.

[3] Middleton, p 215.

[4] Miles, p 205.

[5] Ibid.

[6] Segal, L. (1990) *Slow Motion: Changing masculinities, changing men*, London: Virago, p 317.

[7] French, p 578.

[8] Frank, B. (1993) *Straight/strait jackets for masculinity: Educating for 'real' men*, Atlantis, 18 (1 & 2), p 53.

[9] see Silverstein, O. & Rashbaum, B. (1994) *The Courage to Raise Good Men*, New York: Viking.

[10] French, p 572.

[11] Berg, Rigmor (1990) 'Sexuality: Why Do Women Come Off Second Best?' in N. Grieve & A. Burns (eds) *Australian Women: New Feminist Perspectives*, Melbourne: OUP, p 165.

[12] Segal, L. (1993) 'Sweet sorrows, painful pleasures: Pornography and the perils of heterosexual desire' in L. Segal & M. McIntosh (eds) *Sex Exposed: Sexuality and the Pornography Debate*, New Brunswick, NJ: Rutgers University Press, p 77.

[13] Segal, p 212.

[14] Ibid, pp 213-4.

[15] Lewis, P. M. (1991) 'Mummy, matron and the maids: Feminine presence and absence in male institutions, 1934–63' in M. Roper & J. Tosh (eds) *Manful Assertions: Masculinities in Britain since 1800*, London: Routledge, pp 185–6.

[16] Ward, B. (1992) 'An Interview with Biff Ward' in *Dulwich Centre Newsletter* nos. 3 & 4, p 31.

[17] Carrigan, T., Connell R.W. & Lee, J. (1987) 'Toward a New Sociology of Masculinity' in H. Brod (ed) *The Making of Masculinities: The New Men's Studies*, Cambridge, MA: Unwin Hyman, p 86.

[18] Segal, p 214; Connell, R.W. (1991) 'Live fast and die young: The construction of masculinity among working-class men on the margin of the labour market' in *Australian and New Zealand Journal of Sociology*, 27 (2), p 165; French, p 306.

[19] French, p 323.

[20] Ibid, p 579.

[21] Ibid, p 339.

[22] Ibid, pp 292–3.

[23] Holloway in Middleton, p 190.

Chris McLean
Adelaide, May 2004

Chris McLean is an independent writer and researcher with an interest in how broad social issues impact on people at a personal level.

Natasha Elisabeth Beaumont as Sophie and Gary Day as Jim in the 2004 Sydney Theatre Company production. (Photo: Tracey Schramm)

Amigos was first produced by Sydney Theatre Company at the Drama Theatre, Sydney Opera House, on 8 April 2004, with the following cast:

JIM	Gary Day
DICK	Tony Llewellyn-Jones
STEPHEN	Garry McDonald
HILARY	Wendy Hughes
SOPHIE	Natasha Elisabeth Beaumont

Director, Jennifer Flowers
Set Designer, Michael Scott-Mitchell
Costume Designer, Fiona Crombie
Lighting Designer, David Walters
Composer, Paul Charlier

Characters

JIM

SOPHIE

DICK

HILARY

STEPHEN

ACT ONE

Jim's apartment. Sydney. Evening.

JIM, *mid fifties, stands looking down at Sydney Harbour.* SOPHIE, *mid thirties, looks at him, a frown on her face.*

JIM: Ferries, speedboats, yachts. Always something happening. You know what Captain Phillip said when he first sailed in here? A thousand ships of the line could anchor here. Or something like that.

SOPHIE: Two weeks? You asked them to stay two weeks?

JIM: This Mexican stand-off thing has got to be worked through.

SOPHIE: Fine for you.

JIM: Hilary's okay.

SOPHIE: She's a real sweetie. Practically accused me of ruining your ex-wife's life.

JIM: Annette was her best friend.

SOPHIE: Your ex-wife's never been happier according to that interview she gave. Huge house in Byron Bay—

JIM: Courtesy of me.

SOPHIE: Doing her lithographs and having tantric sex with an advertising dropout ten years younger than she is.

JIM: On my money.

SOPHIE: That bloody ex-wife of yours has landed right on her feet.

JIM: Very rarely on her feet by the sound of it.

SOPHIE: And Hilary has the gall to say that the whole subtext of that interview was a cry of pain! Hour long orgasms? I'll take a little of that sort of pain.

JIM: It wasn't just Annette. Hilary saw you as a threat. Older man, young wife. Dick's surrounded by sexy young theatre nurses every day.

SOPHIE: Then she's still going to feel threatened.

JIM: Frankly, tough luck for her. Dick's my oldest friend .

SOPHIE: I can't co-exist with that woman for two weeks. I can't.

JIM: Try for my sake, honey. Dick and I won an Olympic medal together.

SOPHIE: Relive it in a bar.

JIM: I'll speak to Dick. I'll make it quite clear to him that if they come up to Port Douglas with us, then you're not to be humiliated.

SOPHIE: Sure.

JIM: Sophie, men don't make friends as easily as women. The ones you do hang onto are precious. When the four of us got up on that dais and they put the medals around our necks, and the tears were flowing—that's lifetime bond territory. Unbreakable. And now Roger's dead and Stephen's gone all weird, there's only Dick left. It's really important to me to heal this thing, Sophie. It really is.

SOPHIE: You promise you'll speak to him?

JIM: Absolutely. It'll be great. I was thinking of bringing a top chef up from Sydney to cook for us—

SOPHIE: Jim.

JIM: Yeah, they'd probably resent it. I mean Dick's well off, but he hasn't done nearly as well as I have.

SOPHIE: Mainly because of that dud investment you talked him into, apparently.

JIM: That was a long time back.

SOPHIE: If you *have* to do this, let's keep it simple.

JIM: I'll speak to Dick. It'll be fine.

> SOPHIE *looks at him. Not convinced.*

❖ ❖ ❖ ❖ ❖

SCENE TWO

A city bar. Some days later.

DICK, *the same age as* JIM, *sits at the bar and looks up as* JIM *approaches. They shake hands warmly.*

JIM: When was the last time we did this?

DICK: Too long, mate. Too long.

JIM: Looking well. And happy. Have a good day?

DICK: One of the best.

JIM: Yeah?

DICK: Operated on a six-year-old with heart defects like you wouldn't believe. Blood sloshing around everywhere. Wouldn't've lived more than another couple of years at the most.

JIM: Tough job?

DICK: Never seen anything quite like it. Had to improvise.

JIM: Kid's okay?

DICK: Fine. We were all tense as hell when he came off heart-lung. But off went the heart like clockwork. Pure sinus rhythm up there on the screen. The whole theatre cheered. Students observing up above cheered.

JIM: Great moment.

DICK: The best is walking out to the parents. They're sitting there terrified. White. Trying to read my face. Too scared to speak.

JIM: What do you say?

DICK: 'Mr and Mrs Wallach. I'm very pleased to tell you your son's going to live sixty years longer than he was yesterday.'

JIM: That's awesome.

DICK: He hugs me. She hugs me. And my eardrums are nearly shattering because she's screaming with joy.

JIM: Awesome.

DICK: After a good one like that you're on a high for days afterwards.

JIM: I envy you.

DICK: You make people pretty happy when you decide to invest in their businesses, surely?

JIM: [nodding] I remember you telling me once that it doesn't always work out so well though.

DICK: No. Sometimes the heart doesn't start up again and mum and dad are still out there in the corridor.

JIM: Wouldn't be fun, I guess.

DICK: Lost a kid last week.

JIM: Sorry, mate. You come in feeling like a million bucks and I remind you of a downer. Sorry.

DICK: [*shrugging*] Sometimes you're God, sometimes you're a... lot less than that. [*Pause.*] Hey, look, this holiday—

JIM: You'll come?

DICK: Two weeks? You're sure?

JIM: Absolutely. We'll have a ball. Golf, restaurants—shopping for the girls. Be fantastic.

DICK: Yeah.

JIM: The Amigos ride again. At least two of us do. We'll go to dinner every night and wear our medals.

DICK: Sounds great.

JIM: I want to feel that we're still here for each other, buddy. I know things were difficult when Annette and I broke up.

DICK: Annette was Hilary's very best friend.

JIM: Tell Hilary not to worry. My ex-wife is having a ball.

DICK: Hilary thinks all that bizarre Byron Bay Buddhist stuff is just a scream of pain. 'See, I'm having fun, damn you.' That sort of thing.

JIM: She's screaming a lot, but it ain't pain. I think you're wife's being a little over the top on this issue, frankly.

DICK: It was a shock for her. And me.

JIM: Mate, the thing with Sophie hit me like a train. Nothing I could do. I just worship that kid.

DICK: Yeah.

JIM: Dick, you're my oldest and best friend. Olympic bronze. A canvas off silver. And if the two of us had've been tougher and ditched Roger and maybe even Steve, we would've had gold. Now maybe I acted recklessly, thoughtlessly, in your eyes, in Hilary's eyes, but for me there was absolutely no choice. It had to be. Wham. And I want you to forgive me for that. Because, for me, the kind of history we've had is important.

DICK: It's just. Hilary can be...

JIM: [*nodding*] Yeah.

DICK: Two weeks?

JIM: You can leave early if it's not working out.

DICK: Hilary can be terrific company, but... not if she's tense.

JIM: Yeah, I remember.

DICK: Not if she's tense.

JIM: Look, don't think Sophie doesn't appreciate how difficult it is for Hilary. She said to me just the other day, 'I hope someday I have a friend that's as loyal to me as Hilary is to Annette'.

DICK: Yeah?

JIM: Tell Hilary that.

DICK: She really said that?

JIM: [*nodding*] Sophie's realistic enough to know that she and Hilary are never going to be best buddies, but for our sakes she's going to do everything humanly possible to coexist.

DICK: That's really good.

JIM: She'll be especially sensitive to Hilary's dilemma.

> DICK *nods, but is still patently unsure.*

Dick, this is important. How many real friends do any of us have?

DICK: Sounds like you've got thousands, if we can believe those interviews you give in the business pages.

JIM: Alliances, Dick. Strategic alliances. Not friends.

DICK: Jim, to be frank, none of the disapproval about Sophie is coming from me. I can *totally* understand how you went crazy over her. I mean—*wow*!

JIM: [*nodding*] And she's a lot more than just—*wow*!

DICK: Sure, but *wow*! But I think part of the problem is that Sophie being so... sexy, just makes Hilary madder.

JIM: Yeah, well perhaps Hilary should try and just look a bit beyond the 'wow' stuff. She's a highly intelligent, creative, compassionate and sensitive kid.

DICK: Yeah.

JIM: And warm and funny.

DICK: Sure.

JIM: So maybe you could tell Hilary she's a little more than 'wow'.

DICK: Actually I said, '*Wow*'.

JIM: Yeah, I noticed.

DICK: Lucky dog, is all I can say.

JIM: Let's see if we can make this holiday work, huh? Give it a go.

DICK: [*making a decision*] Okay. Yeah.

JIM: [*slapping him on the back and smiling*] Great. Better get going.

> JIM *shakes* DICK's *hand, turns to go, then turns back.*

Hey, and congratulations on your appointment.

DICK: Oh. That.

JIM: What d'you mean, 'Oh. That.'? It's a great honour.

DICK: Just one more committee.

JIM: A very prestigious committee.

DICK: I don't think anyone takes the honours system very seriously. I didn't when I got mine.

JIM: It still must be good to have.

DICK: If you need to have letters after your name to feel worthwhile you're in a bad way, still…

Tony Llewellyn-Jones (left) as Dick and Gary Day as Jim in the 2004 Sydney Theatre Company production. (Photo: Tracey Schramm)

JIM: I turned one down.

DICK: I heard something to that effect.

JIM: I have to say I kind of regret it now. There's a few people pushing to put me up for it again, I'm told. Hope that won't compromise you.

DICK: If a friend's nomination comes up you leave the room.

JIM: Of course. At any rate, it's not life or death stuff. [*An apparent sudden thought*] Hey, I hope you don't think that this holiday is anything to do with—

DICK: Of *course* not.

JIM: Let's see if we can make this work, huh?

DICK: Yeah. Let's.

> *They embrace. Like bosom buddies.* JIM *turns and leaves.* DICK *watches him go.*

◆ ◆ ◆ ◆ ◆

SCENE THREE

Dick's house. A little later.

HILARY, *early fifties, is inspecting the living room of her Mosman house.* DICK *enters.*

HILARY: Those new cleaners are hopeless.

DICK: Get new ones.

HILARY: If only it was that easy. I could take my pick of fifty personal trainers but finding someone who's actually willing to *work* in this city is impossible. Did you tell Jim we weren't coming?

DICK: It's a beautiful part of the world up there.

HILARY: You told him we'd go?

DICK: I've heard it's a brilliant house.

HILARY: I've heard it's ostentatious beyond belief.

DICK: All glass and light and space. Love that beach design.

HILARY: I've heard it takes you a week to work out the floor plan. You told him we'd go?

DICK: I'd like a bit of relaxation and golf.

HILARY: For two weeks?

DICK: Sophie actually admires the fact you're loyal to Annette.

HILARY: I bet.

DICK: And doesn't expect you'll ever be bosom buddies.

HILARY: How perceptive of her.

DICK: Hilary, he's one of my oldest friends. We won an Olympic medal together.

HILARY: A lot has happened in your life since then. And his.

DICK: He hoped you'd've had time to become a little more accepting.

HILARY: Well, he hopes in vain. I put up with him for years because he's your friend, and Annette was mine, but now he's shacked up with that teenage gold digger—

DICK: I know he can be hard to take sometimes.

HILARY: Sometimes?

DICK: But there's something about him you can't help liking.

HILARY: Precisely what?

DICK: He can be fun. And he never pretends he's a saint.

HILARY: It'd be an extremely hollow pretence.

DICK: He's so blatant sometimes that it's funny. You were right about the real reason we're being invited.

HILARY: It was pretty obvious. The day after you were appointed to the Council the phone rings.

DICK: I had a faint hope it might be genuine, but right at the end he turns and says, 'I hope you don't think… '

HILARY: And you still want to go?

DICK: It's a great holiday spot and he'll wait on us hand and foot.

HILARY: You want him to grovel?

DICK: For *once* he'll have to make some kind of an effort.

HILARY: You want him to grovel?

DICK: No, not grovel, but just for once make an effort. He was probably the worst rower of all four of us back then, but as far as the media were concerned he was the star.

HILARY: Surprise, surprise.

DICK: He got himself invited to all the parties, he got all the women, and as far as the rest of us were concerned, we didn't exist.

HILARY: You want him to grovel.

DICK: [*irritably*] Yes!

HILARY: And you want me to put up with that aerobically honed bimbo so you can watch him grovel.

DICK: In all his press interviews he drops names like he's scattering wedding confetti, and has he ever mentioned me? Or Steve? He didn't even go and see Roger once when he was dying.

HILARY: You only went twice.

DICK: At least I went! Rowing wasn't a sport for him. It was contacts, connections, prestige. The first step of his brilliant career.

HILARY: I think it's sick. You want to accept someone's hospitality when it's obvious you hate him.

DICK: I don't hate him.

HILARY: You should have heard yourself.

DICK: I have issues and old scores. But he's still a friend.

HILARY: So are you going to get him his AC if he does enough grovelling?

DICK: No, fuck him. He was offered an AM a few years back and he turned it down. Had to have the top one because I did.

HILARY: But you'll still pretend that you're doing everything to help?

DICK: He's always been the hare and I've been the tortoise, but the tortoise plodded on and worked quietly and hard and added years to the lives of men who count. And I got an AC. And I'll have the new heart wing of a great Australian hospital named after me in a year's time, so he can just bloody well suffer!

> HILARY *stares at him.*

What?

HILARY: If this is your oldest friend I'd hate to hear you talking about an enemy.

DICK: Things are complicated with men.

HILARY: *Can* you stop him getting an AC?

DICK: Of course.

HILARY: Don't you have to leave the room or something when you're discussing a friend?

Wendy Hughes as Hilary and Tony Llewellyn-Jones as Dick in the 2004 Sydney Theatre Company production. (Photo: Tracey Schramm)

DICK: You do the damage long before that. 'You're his oldest friend, Dick. What's he really like?' 'Frankly, I'm glad I'm his friend and not his enemy.' Then you laughingly tell them some of the things he's told you. They get the message.

HILARY: What's he told you?

DICK: He got drunk one night and said he sees himself as a hawk circling up there in the stratosphere. Hawks have got extraordinary eyesight apparently. They can count the hairs on the back of a mouse from half a mile up. He circles around up there until he spots some hard-working little mouse who's built up a business that's prospering for all the right reasons. Good innovative product. Well managed, well marketed. Jim, and these are his words, slips into a friendly dove disguise and swoops down and whispers into mouse's ear. How he deserves a much bigger house in a much better suburb. A top education for his kids. A holiday house down the coast and, in time, his own business jet. And his new friend, Jim the Investment Banker, has got just the contacts to get him the huge loan he needs to grow his business into the big league. And all goes well, except friendly Jim has done his sums just a little bit better than mouse, who finds he can never quite service his debt. So Good Guy Jim just takes a little more equity and soon Jim owns eighty percent and mouse only twenty. Jim takes mouse out golfing one day and on the eighteenth green says, 'Sorry, buddy, I just sold the business we own at a huge profit, and guess what? Your twenty percent will just cover your debt.'

HILARY: He told you that?

DICK: Proudly. And more. The moment he loves best is when the mouse looks at him and realises he's about to die.

HILARY: That's hideous.

DICK: He said that the Roman Emperor Domitian had gladiators dragged across to him before they had the final coup de grace delivered, because he loved to watch the life drain out of their eyes.

HILARY: Hideous.

DICK: You really think a prick like that *deserves* to be honoured by the community? I *save* lives. Jim destroys them.

HILARY: I can't believe he told you that.

DICK: He was proud. [*Pause.*] It's not so much the glass ceilings that stop women getting corporate power. They're just not so addicted to seeing life drain out of eyes.

HILARY: Dick, we can't go.

DICK: [*resolutely*] I want to.

◆ ◆ ◆ ◆ ◆

SCENE FOUR

Jim's place. The same evening.

SOPHIE *has a cordless phone in her hand.*

SOPHIE: What will I order? Thai, Vietnamese or gourmet?

JIM: I'm hoping one day you'll discover this apartment is equipped with a cooktop and oven.

SOPHIE: The gourmet duck is good.

JIM: Thai.

SOPHIE: [*as she dials*] So are they coming?

JIM: Of course. When would Dick ever knock something back if someone else is paying?

SOPHIE: [*into the phone*] Two gourmet ducks please… 2703. The concierge will let you in if you buzz and come straight up.

    She hangs up.

JIM: Duck is bad for me.

SOPHIE: You're taking anti-cholesterol pills to enjoy life. So enjoy.

JIM: I said Thai.

SOPHIE: Did you tell Dick I won't tolerate being treated like shit by that dragon?

JIM: It won't be a problem.

SOPHIE: Why?

JIM: Hilary read that you're a committee member of that charity that raises money for handicapped kids.

SOPHIE: It's no big deal.

JIM: She's impressed.

SOPHIE: When your brother's got cerebral palsy you appreciate the need.

JIM: She's impressed.

SOPHIE: Dick told you that?

JIM: Absolutely. Hilary works her guts out raising money to help refugees.

SOPHIE: That's *something* in her favour.

JIM: Goes to the camps and everything. Dick doesn't think there'll be a problem.

SOPHIE: Is he going to talk to her?

JIM: Absolutely. Gave me his assurance.

SOPHIE: Sometimes I can't work out whether you lie all the time or only ninety-five percent.

JIM: He's going to talk to her.

SOPHIE: You didn't even ask him.

JIM: I did.

SOPHIE: If you can't sense that this just isn't going to work then you're totally blind.

JIM: Sophie. Listen. I need him to come.

SOPHIE: Why?

JIM: He's just been appointed to the Council of the Order of Australia.

SOPHIE: Which does what?

JIM: Which decides exactly who gets letters after their name and who doesn't.

SOPHIE: I should have realised by now that you don't do things purely out of friendship.

JIM: It's humiliating for me, Sophie. I'm one of this country's great success stories and the best they've offered me is a bloody AM.

SOPHIE: Which most Australians would kill for if I'm not mistaken.

JIM: Dick's got a fucking AC. Fixes a few politicians hearts who should've been left to die, and suddenly he's flavour of the month. There's even talk they're going to name a hospital wing after him.

SOPHIE: Dick's a nice guy.

JIM: What? And I'm a monster? Built the most successful investment bank in the country. Employ hundreds of people.

SOPHIE: You play it hard and you've got a lot of enemies.

JIM: I protect my shareholders!

SOPHIE: Of which you're by far the largest.

JIM: I'm the only key senior figure in Australian finance that hasn't got letters after his name. It's bloody humiliating.

SOPHIE: Dick can't just fix it, surely.

JIM: He can get me over the line. No doubt about it.

SOPHIE: So I've got to put up with freeze face for two weeks.

JIM: Honey, I walk into rooms full of guys who aren't worth pissing on and every one of them's got letters after their name.

SOPHIE: You could have *had* letters.

JIM: If I'm going to have 'em I want the *best*.

SOPHIE: For God's sake, Jim. Everyone knows you're Australia's king of finance.

JIM: [*thumping the table*] Then I want it bloody well acknowledged! You know what we used to call Dick? Dopey Dick. Total loser. A good looking woman would come up and he'd start shaking in terror and speaking some dialect of Swahili. And he's got an AC. How fucking humiliating is that!

SOPHIE: He's a top surgeon.

JIM: A glorified plumber.

SOPHIE: Jim.

JIM: I have to scan a mountain of information and make a hundred decisions a day. And if just two or three of those decisions are wrong—

SOPHIE: You don't have to sell your talent to me. I worked for you.

JIM: [*softening*] This is important to me, Soph. Really important.

SOPHIE: If you think it'll help, let's do it.

JIM: It'll help.

SOPHIE: In your hands he'll be a pushover.

JIM: Don't you believe it. No one spends years of their life getting up at five in the morning and rowing down a freezing river unless there's some killer underneath.

SOPHIE: Dick?

JIM: He's made his good guy act work for him, but he's just as competitive as I am underneath.

SOPHIE: What are you saying? He *won't* help you?

JIM: He will eventually.

SOPHIE: Eventually?

JIM: His AC is the one thing he's got that I haven't. And he'd like to keep it that way.

SOPHIE: How will you change his mind?

JIM: Make sure that *he* knows that *I* know who's responsible if I don't get it.

SOPHIE: Will he care?

JIM: Yep. He's a rabbit. Can't stand people hating him. And I'll make it quite clear how *much* I'll hate him if I don't get it.

SOPHIE: This is going to be one fun holiday.

JIM: It'll be fine. Dick's a rabbit.

SOPHIE: And your good friend.

JIM: I like the guy. I do. But he's never been toughened. Learns to stitch up a few veins and the world loves him. Business is war. And the only people who win wars are warriors.

SOPHIE: My hero Ghengis.

JIM: Better than being a rabbit. Sophie, I've organised a whole truckload of top people to nominate me this year. I want this to happen and I really need your help.

SOPHIE: Have I ever refused?

JIM: Where's that fucking duck? Call 'em again.

◆ ◆ ◆ ◆ ◆

SCENE FIVE

Jim and Sophie's house. Port Douglas. A month later.

HILARY *looks around the high, vaulted ceilings and glass walls and out at the view.* DICK *appears and looks around also. They look at each other and raise their eyebrows.*

HILARY: Found your way back from the toilet?

DICK: [*laughing*] Took a while.

HILARY: Modular design. Here a wing, there a wing, everywhere a wing wing.

DICK: [*laughing*] Checked out the gallery? Some great paintings.

HILARY: Was that a Davida Allen or does some relative's kid fingerpaint?

DICK: Did you see the charming Imants Tiller with the characteristic oil can up the bum.

HILARY: [*nodding*] Money no object, pretentiousness obligatory.

DICK: [*putting an arm around* HILARY] Love, this is going to be awful. You were quite right, we shouldn't've come. I'm sorry.

HILARY: I've dragged you off to some appalling places in my time.

DICK: Iquitos.

HILARY: The brochures waxed lyrical about the upper reaches of the Amazon.

DICK: But not the piranhas, anacondas, ribbon fish, bird-eating tarantulas, and the monkey that got amorous with you in our tent.

HILARY: I thought you'd had a rush of blood.

DICK: I'll think of an excuse to get us out of here.

> *He gives her an affectionate squeeze.* JIM *enters carrying a champagne bottle, followed by* SOPHIE *with fluted champagne glasses. She pours champagne as the conversation continues.*

JIM: Unpacked?

DICK: Sure have.

HILARY: What a house, Jim. It's magnificent.

JIM: Sophie worked hand in hand with the architect. It was her vision.

SOPHIE: Jim's exaggerating. It was ninety-five percent Gabriel Poole.

JIM: There's still a lot of you in it, Sophie.

SOPHIE: I'm really happy with the result.

DICK: You should be. It's fantastic.

> DICK *puts his arm around* SOPHIE *and gives her an affectionate squeeze.* HILARY *isn't impressed.*

SOPHIE: From here on in, just treat the place like your own and enjoy yourselves.

DICK: We will.

SOPHIE: Have a seat.

JIM: [*raising his champagne glass*] To friendship. The glue of life.

They all mutter 'to friendship'. There's a silence.

DICK: I love the spaces, the shapes, the light. The view.

JIM: You work hard all your life, I figure it's got to be for something.

HILARY: How are the children, Jim?

JIM: Simon just got promoted to chief analyst at Salomon's. Can you believe that? Kid's twenty-four and he's in New York practically running the world. We were a bit worried about Francesca because she wasn't 'academic', but she's taken to fashion like a duck to water.

DICK: Fashion? Last time I heard she was—

JIM: She switched to fashion. Designing her own label and making money by the fistful. And she *loves* London. Well, not so much London as the proximity to Europe. She said she finally realised that the thing that was really depressing her here was the total lack of cultural and artistic history.

HILARY: A bit of an overstatement.

JIM: [*shrugging*] Italy's her favourite. She'll probably end up living in Rome. Already speaks fluent Italian.

DICK: Really?

JIM: Huge relief. I was really worried about those two when they were in their teens, but they've really surprised me.

HILARY: Annette was a wonderful mother.

JIM: Your Grant? Got over his problems?

HILARY: He's fine.

JIM: Pulled out of his little trough?

DICK: Never seen him better.

JIM: Medication worked?

DICK: [*nodding*] Going back to finish his Law degree.

JIM: Glad to hear it. Great to *want* to be a writer, but in the real world there are thousands of books published that hardly anyone wants to read.

HILARY: When your child is highly motivated to do something it's natural to want to offer support.

JIM: Absolutely. It's just that 'being creative' has been oversold to this generation when the fact is the world's drowning in bloody creativity. Six new film reviews every day.

DICK: He's really back on track.

HILARY: He hasn't given up his aspirations. He's just being realistic at this point in time.

JIM: John Grisham used his legal background to become hugely successful.

HILARY: I don't think Grant's trying to write like John Grisham.

JIM: He could do worse. Great craftsman.

HILARY: His characters are cardboard.

JIM: For sixty million US a year I'd write cardboard. For that money I'd *eat* cardboard.

DICK: Things pretty tricky in your game at the moment, Jim?

JIM: Having my best year ever.

DICK: Great.

JIM: Got super firms lining up to throw money at me. In tough times they come straight to the people with the proven track records. Economy doesn't effect your trade I guess. Arteries keep clogging up.

DICK: Yep.

SOPHIE: With your reputation I guess you'd have more patients than you can handle.

DICK: I do.

JIM: They do keep stats these days, don't they? Each doctor's mortality rate?

DICK: Yeah. They do—

JIM: I guess your stats are right up there on top.

DICK: Stats don't mean everything. The best take on the chanciest cases.

JIM: Of course.

HILARY: Even so, Dick's rate is very low.

JIM: Top of his game.

DICK: Like you are in yours. Hawk eye.

JIM: What?

DICK: Way up there looking for a fat, little mouse.

JIM: It's not like that.

DICK: That's what you told me.

JIM: When did I say that?

DICK: One night when you'd had the odd sherbet.

JIM: [*shaking his head*] No.

DICK: You said you swoop down on mouse and plant dreams. 'One day you will fly in your own corporate jet.'

JIM: I can't remember any of that hawk shit?

DICK: You said it, mate. You said it.

JIM: I don't see myself as a predator. I develop partnerships.

DICK: Glad to hear you've changed.

JIM: Dreams are what drives the world. If you don't want something badly, you may as well be dead.

HILARY: Buddhists say that ridding yourself of material desires is the only way to true happiness.

JIM: Frankly, that's horseshit. Who's going to be happy sitting round chanting 'Ommmm' all their life. Apart from my wife.

SOPHIE: Your ex-wife.

HILARY: She does seem happy.

JIM: She can afford to sit around under banyan trees with her dropout beach bum. I provide the cash.

HILARY: Not quite a beach bum. He was creative director of a huge advertising agency before he realised it wasn't what he wanted in life.

JIM: Yeah, well I've done a bit of checking on Tantric Tony. He was given the flick because he hadn't come up with an original idea in twenty years.

HILARY: He had burnout. He admits it, but on the other hand he's charming, handsome, witty and incredibly well read.

JIM: I'm currently paying for his erudition.

HILARY: The important thing from my point of view is that he's made Annette very happy.

JIM: I thought you said her happiness act was just a 'cry of pain'.

HILARY: [*shaking her head*] When I saw them together on the way up here it's obvious that she's truly happy for the first time in her life.

JIM: My heart sings. Look, I've had a heavy couple of weeks. I think I'll crash early tonight. Golf tomorrow, Dick?

DICK: I think I might just sit around and read.

JIM: [*as he gets up*] Sorry, Hilary, but I just can't hack people who
  don't want to achieve something in life. You really think Dick
  should've sat round all his life dreaming of Ying and Yang. Tell that
  to the thousands of patients he's given years of life to.

HILARY: Different people find different types of fulfilment.

JIM: Personally I'm glad Dick and I *did* something with our lives. Not
  wasted them like Stephen and Roger.

HILARY: Wasted is a pretty strong assessment.

JIM: Those two had an Olympic medal and the world at their feet. Okay,
  Roger was gay. That's fine. One of my best young analysts is gay.
  But he doesn't go out every night and try and have sex with a football
  team.

HILARY: He got AIDS before they knew it was a virus.

JIM: He told Steve that he'd had sex with way over a thousand guys.
  You're telling me that's not self destructive?

HILARY: We might think it is. He didn't.

JIM: He was potential CEO material. And Steve. First class honours
  degree in maths. Top job as an actuary. And like your son he decides
  he's going to be 'creative'. And unlike your son he doesn't think
  twice. Well, he's been writing away for fifteen years now in a tin
  shack down south on welfare, and nothing he's done's ever appeared
  on a bookstand.

HILARY: It's his choice.

JIM: Some choice. My pride wouldn't let me ever sink that low. Help
  yourselves to drinks. I'm having an early night.

  He goes. There's a silence.

SOPHIE: I think I'll have an early night too.

  She goes. HILARY *and* DICK *sit there, then look at each other.*

DICK: I thought you were going to try and be civil.

HILARY: Civil's one thing. Draping your bloody arms all over that woman's
  another.

  She gets up and walks off.

◆ ◆ ◆ ◆ ◆

SCENE SIX

Jim and Sophie's bedroom. A minute later.

JIM *sits on the end of the bed as* SOPHIE *enters.*

SOPHIE: You've blown your AC now.

JIM: Hilary was deliberately provoking me. She's still thick as thieves with Annette.

SOPHIE: So what?

JIM: Annette obviously recruited her to rub it in about how deliriously happy she is with that deadbeat dropout.

SOPHIE: So what? You're married to me now.

JIM: Tony's 'well read'. Well hung more like it.

SOPHIE: What does it matter?

JIM: She just loves rubbing my nose in it.

SOPHIE: Okay, it's just possible your ex-wife is having better sex with Tony than she ever had with you. Is it a problem?

JIM: Yes, because it's not true! We had great sex. At least for the first fifteen years. And if things got stale after that it's her fault.

SOPHIE: Jim.

JIM: When all the women's magazines started wittering on about multiple orgasms Annette said, 'What's all the fuss? I've always had them.'

SOPHIE: Jim, you're brilliant in the bedroom, but it just might be that there is another who approaches your levels of virtuosity. Okay?

JIM: A few weeks back she's in pain, now she's blissfully happy.

SOPHIE: She's supposed to be part of your past.

JIM: Hour-long orgasms! What bullshit. She'd have heart failure. And Dick needling me with all the hawk and mouse stuff. I never said that.

SOPHIE: One night when you were drunk you told me exactly the same thing.

JIM: He thinks he's got the whip hand now so he can say anything.

SOPHIE: Frankly, I think he was provoked. Did you have to do all that boasting?

JIM: Boasting?

SOPHIE: How *hugely* successful your children are. How the whole world is lining up to throw dollars at you.

JIM: Am I supposed to pretend my kids are screwed-up losers like theirs is?

SOPHIE: You paid a fortune to get your daughter started in fashion and you pulled every string in the book to get your son started in New York.

JIM: You can open doors for them but then they're on their own. And the big boys *are* lining up to throw money at me, because I'm the best.

SOPHIE: Just keep on behaving like you are now and there's no earthly hope you'll ever get letters after your name.

JIM: I ditch a wife, my two children still barely speak to me, and all I am to you is a 'boaster'.

SOPHIE: Jim, don't lay the blame about your children on me.

JIM: I'm not blaming you. I made the decision to leave my wife.

SOPHIE: Yes you did. You seemed very adamant about it at the time if you remember.

JIM: I just didn't think they'd be so negative. I thought they might try and understand.

Natasha Elisabeth Beaumont as Sophie and Gary Day as Jim in the 2004 Sydney Theatre Company production. (Photo: Tracey Schramm)

SOPHIE: If you're so cut up about your children, go back to your bloody wife.

JIM: She's got Tony.

SOPHIE: You *want* to go back to her?

JIM: Exactly what am I getting out of this relationship?

SOPHIE: About as much as I am.

JIM: Just spare yourself a thought about the lifestyle you lead.

SOPHIE: I don't need all this.

JIM: Any other woman in Australia would kill for it.

SOPHIE: They're welcome.

> *She storms off into the ensuite.*

❖ ❖ ❖ ❖ ❖

SCENE SEVEN

A bedroom in the other wing.

HILARY *has just come out of the ensuite in her bathrobe.* DICK *is sitting on the bed.* HILARY *is simmering with anger.*

HILARY: Francesca a wonderful success in the fashion industry? Sure, because Daddy tried to buy her affection back by paying a fortune for a label. Why didn't you support me about Grant?

DICK: I did.

HILARY: It was obvious that you were hugely relieved he's back doing Law.

DICK: I haven't got millions to throw at him like Jim.

HILARY: We would have had a lot more to throw if you hadn't gone into that stupid investment with him.

DICK: Jim lost a fortune too.

HILARY: He could afford to. Going in with him as an equal partner was insanity. No, it was worse than that. It was my dick's as big as your dick territory.

DICK: Nobody could've predicted the property market was going to nosedive like that.

HILARY: Well, it did and we were ten years paying back our debt. We're not staying here another day.

DICK: We can't just walk out.

HILARY: Think of some excuse. And if you ever let that man get an AC it's over between us.

DICK: I told you. There's no way he's ever going to get one.

HILARY: In that case it's sick you being here.

DICK: All right, I'll think of an excuse.

HILARY: Do you want to sleep here or in the adjoining mini wing?

DICK: I thought maybe, given it's a holiday, we might even share a bed.

HILARY: And have you heaving away on top of me pretending I'm that bimbo. Stay right there.

She exits next door. DICK *sighs.*

◆ ◆ ◆ ◆ ◆

SCENE EIGHT

The living room. Next morning.

JIM *is reading the paper.* DICK *enters.*

JIM: Sleep well?

DICK: No.

JIM: Really? I always do up here. The rhythmic crashing of the waves.

DICK: Kept me awake.

JIM: Takes a day or so to unwind. Breakfast stuff's out on the deck. Sophie's gone for her morning walk on the beach.

DICK: Jim, I think we might have to—

JIM: Mate, it's going to be fine. I stuffed things up last night. Going on and on about how brilliant my kids are.

DICK: You have given them quite a bit of help.

JIM: Yeah, and the truth is they still barely talk to me. Paid a fortune to get Francesca in the fashion business and she was still so vile last time she was here I had to tell her to pack her bags and get out.

DICK: Yeah?

JIM: Treated Sophie like shit.

DICK: You must've known there was going to be resentment.

JIM: Yeah, but it still hurts. Simon still won't even meet Sophie.

DICK: That's pretty rough.

JIM: [*shaking his head*] So please take last night in the context of the fact that I've probably lost their affection forever.

DICK: They'll come round.

JIM: One lives in hope. And sorry about what I said about young Grant. If he wants to write novels that don't necessarily sell a million, then good luck to him. He's got integrity.

DICK: Truth is I'm really glad he's back doing Law. I sneaked a look at some of the stuff he'd written that he showed his mother. It might be brilliant, but I just didn't get it.

JIM: I try and read some of those prize-winning novels Sophie reads and I can't get past the first ten pages.

DICK: I'm the same.

JIM: Did you try that one about the kid in the boat with the tiger that talks? Won every prize going.

DICK: Missed that one.

JIM: Pathetic. And look, I didn't mean to carry on about how well I'm doing. I still feel guilty about letting you come in on that office block development.

DICK: You lost a heap too.

JIM: It was just bad luck. I thought the market might drop, but not that much.

DICK: You pointed out the risks.

JIM: If we had've hung on four years or so we would've been laughing today.

DICK: I couldn't afford to.

JIM: Yeah. Dick, I know how much it hurt you and I really have felt bad.

DICK: I was the one who kept asking you to let me know if there was a good investment on the horizon.

JIM: Yeah, but I shouldn't have got you to borrow that sort of money.

DICK: It's a long time ago now.

JIM: I hope everything's fine now. Financially.

DICK: Yeah.

JIM: Good. Important to be secure.

DICK: I'm not as secure as you, but okay.

JIM: You know something? I've got everything I need, but when I think back to the old days, I feel... a sense... of loss.

DICK: Me too.

JIM: God, we were alive back then, weren't we? Didn't know it, took it for granted, squandered it, but we were. I try and pretend life's still a ball, but the truth is the great days are gone and making money sometimes feels like a kind of... compensation. Do you ever feel like that?

DICK: Ever? Try every day.

JIM: Truth is, sometimes I miss it more than I can bear. Remember the Village in Mexico City? You'd see a gorgeous Lithuanian high jumper or whatever and say, 'I'm having her'. And chances were you did.

DICK: You did.

JIM: You did okay.

DICK: Better than now.

JIM: Things not so good? With you and Hilary?

DICK: We get on fine on day to day stuff.

JIM: Other stuff?

DICK: Once a month. If I'm lucky.

JIM: And that's enough?

DICK: No.

JIM: Hey, remember that Bulgarian gymnast? You were going to marry her. We had to drag you away.

DICK: I got a bit carried away, didn't I?

JIM: Fabulous times. We were kings of the world.

DICK: *You* still are.

JIM: You're not poor.

DICK: Sophie, mate. 'Yow.'

JIM: Can you maybe refer to her without saying 'Wow' or 'Yow'?

DICK: Sorry, mate. She reminds me of someone. Can't think who.

JIM: You're still at the top of your game, you're earning big money, there'd be oodles of women like Sophie around.

DICK: I did fall in love a few years back. Research physiologist I met at a conference.

JIM: Nice?

DICK: Gorgeous. And I kind of knew it was my last chance.

JIM: So?

DICK: Couldn't do it.

JIM: Yeah, it's tough to contemplate losing half of everything you own.

DICK: [*getting passionate*] It wasn't the money. I just didn't want to hurt Hilary. But now… I look at Sophie and think maybe I should've.

JIM: Well, don't.

DICK: Don't?

JIM: Sophie was the best PA I ever had, and I should've had the sense to leave it that way.

DICK: You're kidding.

JIM: We were the perfect team. I'd do the cut and thrust and she'd do the backup. And stroke my ego. That's what I fell for. 'You handled him brilliantly.' 'You sure put the fear of God in him.' We all need a cheer squad, me more than most. But marry your cheer leader and she's suddenly on an equal footing and it's hell. They tell you that in management school. Never ever marry your PA. Did I listen? No, Jim, you didn't and now it's nightmare time.

DICK: With Sophie?

JIM: Sweet, compliant PA suddenly becomes Sophie ball buster. You married your theatre nurse and look what happened to you.

DICK: Apart from the sex, Hilary and I get on fine.

JIM: The only thing working for Sophie and me *is* the sex. [*He sighs.*] You know something? The sex drive is a disaster. Everything else you can be rational about, but sex makes you obsessed with the wrong person in the wrong place at the wrong time and your life goes to shit. Why does Hilary hate me so much? It's not just about Annette and Sophie. She's shitty about the Stephen thing too, isn't she?

DICK: Yeah, and I have to say I wasn't thrilled about it either.

JIM: There was no *way* I was going to give him a hundred thousand dollars. And you were crazy to. You'll never get it back.

DICK: You were in a much better position to give it than I was.

JIM: You're crazy. You'll never see a dollar of it again.

DICK: I couldn't say no. In the circumstances.

JIM: You're a sucker for the hard luck story, Dick. You were going to marry that damn ugly Bulgarian so she didn't have to go back behind the Iron Curtain.

DICK: For fuck's sake, his kid was dying, mate. He was desperate.

JIM: The money was *never* going to help.

DICK: The four of us were inseparable once. You can't just wipe all that history out.

JIM: Stephen is a loony loser. And that's not my fault or my responsibility. What's happened to your hundred thousand? Snapped up by some quack in the US. Thank you very much.

DICK: Stephen thought it was his only hope.

JIM: Well, he should've done some basic research like I did. The guy was a total fake and you've thrown your money away.

DICK: Frankly, I think you behaved like a bastard.

JIM: How come you suddenly found yourself on the Honours Council, Dick?

DICK: What are you suggesting?

JIM: When Malcolm rang you and asked if you'd be one of my referees—

DICK: I said yes.

JIM: You said it was a funny coincidence, but you'd just been offered a place on the Council but were going to turn it down. You were far too busy heading up the fund raising committee for your new heart wing. Then three days later you ring back and say you can't referee me because you'd decided to accept. Don't need to be a genius to work out what's going on there.

DICK: You really think I accepted so I could stop you getting an honour?

JIM: You know something? I do. You knew you shouldn't have given that hundred thousand. You know I was right.

DICK: [*angrily*] How do you say no to an old friend whose son's about to die?!

JIM: You tell him the truth. He's being conned.

DICK: It was his only fucking ray of hope!

JIM: You've got a whole litany of resentments, haven't you? I warned you time and time again that the property investment was speculative, but you *had* to have a part of the action. You thought it was all so easy. Money for nothing. Now it's revenge time.

DICK: You're paranoid.

JIM: Why did you suddenly decide to go on a committee you didn't want to be on?

DICK: Because the Minister rang me again and said he'd really like me on it, and I did his bypass and I liked him. Nothing sinister at all.

JIM: Oh, yeah.

DICK: Look, I *was* bitter about the investment. You warned me, sure, but you could've said don't be bloody stupid and risk a loan that size.

JIM: I did!

DICK: And a hundred thousand for Stephen was small change for you. But none of that means I would deliberately sabotage your bloody honour. I'll do everything I can to get the nomination through.

JIM: Really?

DICK: Of course.

JIM: [*with a sigh*] I don't know why getting those letters means so much to me. But they do. It's driving me crazy. I guess that before you die you want your community to say you were worth something. It's meant something to you, hasn't it?

DICK: Yeah.

JIM: And time's running out. I can't stay at the top of the tree much longer. Not like you.

DICK: What do you think? What I do is stress free?

JIM: No, but—

DICK: Halfway through a tough one I'm starting to shake. The tension is huge.

JIM: Try waiting for the other side to crack when there's a hundred million at stake.

DICK: You can cope a lot better than me. Before a big race I'd be out the back vomiting and you'd be happily chatting up some bird. I just want to get the money raised for the new wing and get out while I'm ahead.

JIM: Good for you.

DICK: The real reason I didn't leave Hilary for the physiologist was I didn't want her to see how much I was starting to stress out. Hilary at least understands.

JIM: Did you mean it? You'll help me?

DICK: Yes, but it doesn't mean I don't think you're a prick.

JIM: Okay, I should've given Stephen the money.

DICK: Didn't even visit Roger when he was dying.

JIM: It's not because he was gay.

DICK: Come on. You reacted like a scalded cat when you found out in Mexico.

JIM: It was a shock.

DICK: You didn't visit him because he was gay.

JIM: Those photos of those gay skeletons dying. Couldn't hack it.

DICK: He was really hurt. *Really* hurt.

JIM: Okay, I *am* disgusted at gayness. Gay marriages, holding hands in public, kissing in close-up on our television screens— [*He shudders.*] Anyrate, you only went once.

DICK: Three times.

JIM: So you should've. You were one of his ex's.

DICK: Hey!

JIM: You rooted him.

DICK: Once or twice.

JIM: Here we are in training for the biggest event of our lives and I walk in and you're chockas. No wonder we only got bloody bronze.

DICK: It didn't do anything for me and I've never done it since.

JIM: [*screwing up his face in disgust*] I can still see it.

DICK: You don't have to keep bringing it up.

JIM: The Four Amigos? Jesus.

DICK: The real reason you didn't see him is he just wasn't important enough. Like Steve isn't important enough.

JIM: Steve is a dropout beach bum. Why do you persist with these sentimental attachments to losers?

DICK: Because I still like them.

JIM: [*with a sigh*] Okay. I'm a bastard. Always have been. If you don't support me in the Council I'll only be getting what I deserved.

DICK: [*irritated*] I've said I'll support you and I will.

JIM: Even though I'm a bastard?

DICK: You've always been a bastard.

JIM: Mate, I don't deserve a friend like you.

DICK: I know.

JIM: [*putting an arm around* DICK*'s shoulder*] I really don't. Now let's hit golf balls.

> DICK *sighs and is led out by* JIM *with his arm on his shoulder.*

DICK: I wanted to read!

JIM: This course is a pearl. Greg Norman design.

◆ ◆ ◆ ◆ ◆

SCENE NINE

The kitchen. Some time later.

SOPHIE *is working in the kitchen.* HILARY *comes in from the beach.*

HILARY: Beautiful on the beach.

SOPHIE: Perfect day. Usually is this time of year.

HILARY: Men gone?

SOPHIE: [*nodding*] Golf I guess.

HILARY: Only known game where the lowest score wins.

SOPHIE: If it was the other way I'd be a champion.

HILARY: You play?

SOPHIE: Hate the game.

HILARY: Me too. Can I do something?

SOPHIE: It's just a salad. I'm almost finished. [*Pause.*] So glad to hear how happy Annette is now.

HILARY: It's taken quite a while.

SOPHIE: I'm going to write to her.

HILARY: Would that be wise?

SOPHIE: I understand she was distressed, but she did make some accusations against me that I'd like to put right.

HILARY: Mightn't it stir things up again?

SOPHIE: Frankly, I don't care. I didn't actually pursue Jim. I wanted to be his PA, but that was it. That was it.

HILARY: Even if it's true, I'm not sure Annette would want to believe it.

SOPHIE: I'd like to tell her whether she believes it or not. He was charismatic, assured, funny and brilliant at business politics, and I was impressed. But I want her to know that if he hadn't really pursued me, and I mean *really* pursued me, I wouldn't have let it happen. But it did happen and I did fall in love in a big way, but in case she thinks it's been brilliant from that moment on, it hasn't. I'm glad she's happy because I'm not sure I am.

HILARY: Really?

SOPHIE: What I didn't realise, and I'm sure she does, is that Jim can tolerate acolytes, but not equals.

HILARY: You didn't realise what you were getting?

SOPHIE: [*shaking her head*] No.

HILARY: I'm sure there are compensations.

    She looks around at the house.

Natasha Elisabeth Beaumont (left) as Sophie and Wendy Hughes as Hilary in the 2004 Sydney Theatre Company production. (Photo: Tracey Schramm)

SOPHIE: You think I've got everything I could possibly want?

HILARY: I don't think anybody has.

SOPHIE: Did you and Dick both want a child?

HILARY: I did, very much.

SOPHIE: And I'm sure you're glad you did?

HILARY: Very much. Grant mighn't be so glamorously brilliant as Jim's two, but I love him dearly.

SOPHIE: A child was part of my deal with Jim. Then suddenly 'no child'. It would upset his 'other children' far too much. Why? They're scared my kid might get part of the loot. Fine if they practically spit in my face, but they can never ever be 'upset'.

HILARY: You don't have to stay married.

SOPHIE: I'm not.

HILARY: Really?

SOPHIE: [*indicating the house*] You think I'm so wedded to all this I'll stay at all costs?

HILARY: I think it couldn't help being a factor.

SOPHIE: Why do you feel entitled to feel so superior to me?

HILARY: I don't.

SOPHIE: You were the nurse who married the surgeon. I was the PA who married the boss. And we're both miserable.

HILARY: What makes you feel entitled to make that judgement?

SOPHIE: Separate beds on a holiday?

HILARY: You checked?

SOPHIE: I went up to give you fresh towels.

HILARY: [*angrily*] How the hell can a couple expect to keep the sexual thing at full throttle after thirty years? Just because you used sex to get what you wanted doesn't mean we're all obsessed with it.

SOPHIE: You think you know what I am, but you don't.

HILARY: What exactly are you?

SOPHIE: Someone who had a far tougher time than you did as a kid for a start.

HILARY: My parents weren't wealthy.

SOPHIE: Wealthy enough to send you to one of the best schools in the country.

HILARY: They worked hard to do that.

SOPHIE: My mother worked hard too. Problem was she had no husband and four kids, one of whom had severe cerebral palsy.

HILARY: You've clearly won on the childhood misery stakes. I would've thought that'd make it even harder to leave all this.

SOPHIE: If I leave Jim, I won't be poor.

HILARY: Of course. You'll get a big divorce settlement.

SOPHIE: I won't need one.

HILARY: You'll just go back to being a PA?

SOPHIE: I'm wealthy independent of Jim.

HILARY: You must have saved an awful lot when you were a PA?

SOPHIE: I worked at other things before that. And invested well.

HILARY: You must've. We'll leave shortly.

SOPHIE: I wouldn't've thought there's much reason to stay.

HILARY: Jim and Dick have been friends for a long while.

SOPHIE: Do you belong to a book club?

HILARY: Yes.

SOPHIE: All women?

HILARY: Yes. Why?

SOPHIE: Mine too. I said to Jim, 'Why don't men have book clubs?' He looked absolutely horrified. 'You think I'm going to spend hours reading a book and working out what it's about, then have some other prick try and ram his ideas down my throat?'

HILARY: Are you making a point about men or Jim?

SOPHIE: Both.

HILARY: Are you saying Jim and Dick *aren't* good friends?

SOPHIE: It hasn't occurred to you that this holiday has an agenda? Something to do with Dick being appointed to the Awards Council?

HILARY: Jim would surely realise that Dick would disqualify himself from discussing Jim.

SOPHIE: I'm not sure Jim would.

HILARY: I know my husband extremely well after all these years and there's no way he'd consider any special favours.

SOPHIE: He seems to like suggesting he might.

HILARY: What are you saying?

SOPHIE: He seems to be enjoying being in a position of power.

HILARY: Are you suggesting Dick is gloating?

SOPHIE: You haven't noticed?

HILARY: I know my husband extremely well and it's not in his nature.

SOPHIE: Must be very comforting to know a husband so well.

HILARY: Are you suggesting I don't?

SOPHIE: Not as well as you think.

HILARY: You know something about him that I don't?

SOPHIE: The reason I've got money is that I worked my way through business college. At the very top end of the market.

> HILARY *stares at her.*

Don't worry. Your husband won't recognise me. I was only one of many he employed. And I used a lot of make-up and the baby doll look. Pout and all. [*She assumes a breathy French accent.*] And I spoke like this. He loved it.

> HILARY *continues to stare.*

I'm very grateful to him. He was one of the main reasons I'm financially secure.

> HILARY *turns, shocked, to go.*

And if you tell one soul what I've just told you, the whole world gets to hear about Dick.

HILARY: There is no way Jim is *ever* going to get an AC.

SOPHIE: He never was, was he?

> HILARY *storms outside.* SOPHIE *picks up the salad and empties it into the kitchen tidy. She picks up a book and heads off in the opposite direction to* HILARY. *There are a few seconds of silence, then a man in his fifties appears wearing very well-worn beach clothes. He's carrying a manuscript of some kind in his hands. He looks around at the opulence and whistles in surprise. He puts down the manuscript, pours himself a drink, then relaxes into a large chair.*

END OF ACT ONE

ACT TWO

SCENE ONE

Jim's living room. Some time later.

SOPHIE *comes in from outside, putting on a shirt. She doesn't see the new arrival who's fallen fast asleep in his chair, until she practically falls over his feet. She gives a shriek of alarm which wakes him up. From this point on he's clearly on the edge. Manic, almost out of control.*

SOPHIE: Who the hell are you?

STEPHEN: Stephen. Sorry.

SOPHIE: Stephen who?

STEPHEN: Stephen Ryan. I used to . . .

> *He makes rowing motions with his arms.*

SOPHIE: Oh. Stephen Ryan? One of the Amigos?

STEPHEN: Yeah. I only live about a hundred ks south of here and I heard Jim and Dick were up here and I needed to see them so I caught the bus up.

SOPHIE: Oh.

STEPHEN: Sorry if I startled you, but the doors were open and no one was here.

SOPHIE: That's fine. They're both out at the moment. Playing golf.

> STEPHEN *makes a golf swinging motion with his arms.*

STEPHEN: Always wanted to try that. Looks easy when Tiger Woods does it, but I guess it's not.

SOPHIE: It's not. Like a drink?

STEPHEN: [*holding up a glass of water*] It's fine. I got some water.

> HILARY *walks in from the patio.*

HILARY: Stephen. What are you doing here?

STEPHEN: Have to see Dick and Jim.

HILARY: So sorry to hear about your son.

STEPHEN: Yeah.

HILARY: How are you coping?

STEPHEN: Not so well.

SOPHIE: Your son died?

HILARY: Didn't Jim tell you?

SOPHIE: No.

STEPHEN: No reason he should. I'm just a very minor blip on Jim's radar these days.

SOPHIE: How old was he?

STEPHEN: Twenty-three.

SOPHIE: I'm so sorry.

STEPHEN: Yeah. Makes you feel life is kind of senseless. You read Richard Dawkins?

HILARY & SOPHIE: [*together*] No.

STEPHEN: He says we're all random results of blind evolution. He says the universe is devoid of purpose. Devoid of meaning. Pitiless. When you're grasping for some kind of… understanding, it's not exactly comforting.

HILARY & SOPHIE: [*together*] No.

STEPHEN: He seems to find a kind of magnificent grandeur in it all, but maybe he's never had a kid die.

SOPHIE: Sorry. I don't know what to say.

STEPHEN: Say anything. The worst thing for me is people say nothing.

SOPHIE: It must have been awful.

HILARY: For a parent it's your worst nightmare.

STEPHEN: It was. Still is. But in another way it was incredibly rich and moving. We'd never been all that close, Daniel and I. I'd left the marriage when he was still pretty young and always felt guilty about it and he'd always felt abandoned. When his mother died it left the kid pretty much alone and as I found out, desperate for the love I'd never given him. Sorry, I didn't mean here to come here and rabbit on about this.

HILARY & SOPHIE: [*together*] It's fine.

STEPHEN: I mean, the death itself was horrible. Jesus, don't ever believe those stories you hear when they say so and so died 'peacefully'. Well, maybe some people do, but with Daniel it was horrible. The look of fear on his face. Horrible. Sorry. I'm rattling on. Can't stop myself.

HILARY: If it helps, please do.

SOPHIE: Absolutely.

STEPHEN: It's so hard to find someone to listen.

SOPHIE: If it helps, please do.

HILARY: Absolutely.

STEPHEN: It's like you've got to know this kid better than you ever thought you would or that you've ever got a right to, and you don't want the memory of what he was to ever die. I mean, you know it will. You know that a hundred years down the track no one will know that *any* of us ever existed, but you want to fight this stubborn rearguard action for him. Keep telling people he was here. I feel that if I don't do it, then it'll somehow be as if he never lived at all. Sorry, I just can't shut up.

SOPHIE: Say whatever you want.

STEPHEN: [*shaking his head*] You haven't even met me, and suddenly this crazy guy lands in your living room.

HILARY: Stephen, I've known you forever. Say whatever you want.

SOPHIE: Whatever you want.

STEPHEN: It's weird what this's done to me. Hilary can tell you that of all the Amigos I was the least Amigo-ish. It was all you could do to get me to say a sentence, right Hilary?

HILARY: You certainly weren't as talkative as Roger or Jim.

STEPHEN: One journalist suggested we be renamed the Three Amigos plus Sphinx.

HILARY: You were quiet, but I always thought you were courteous and charming.

STEPHEN: You must have been good at reading body language. But now I can't keep my mouth shut. A couple of weeks before he died Daniel looked at me and said, 'Dad, let it out. If you're feeling something, tell me.' The tears started rolling out of my eyes, but I still couldn't let it out. He got angry and said, 'For fuck's sake, Dad, say it. Whatever it is, say it. What are you feeling?'. I said, 'I'm feeling that I love you, but I don't have a clue how to say it'. And he said, 'You've just said it. It's taken me nearly twenty-four years to ever hear it, but you've just said it.' And we cried and hugged each other for the very first time in our lives. And from that moment it's just like the floodgates have opened. If I feel something, out it comes. Sphinx to Oprah Winfrey. I'm a menace. No one can shut me up.

HILARY: It's healthy.

STEPHEN: There's a lot of anger to let out. That's what the grief books say. Mountains of it. Why you've been singled out. Why not someone else. The sheer randomness of it. The lack of fairness. We've got this thing that life should somehow be fair. And when it isn't it sort of knocks us sideways. Have you read Samuel Beckett?

HILARY: No.

SOPHIE: No.

STEPHEN: I'm reading everything I can to try and make sense of things.

Garry McDonald as Stephen and Wendy Hughes as Hilary in the 2004 Sydney Theatre Company production. (Photo: Tracey Schramm)

HILARY: I saw a Beckett play once and it was pretty grim.

STEPHEN: *Waiting for Godot*?

HILARY: Yes.

STEPHEN: [*nodding*] Waiting for Godot is a metaphor for waiting to die. Sometimes I think Sam Beckett was the only truly honest man that ever lived. He knew life is equal parts pain and boredom. The sugarcoaters say Sam was just a bitter, old pessimist. Life is about connection, they chant. Connection with others. Sure. Then they die and you go crazy with grief. Sorry, just a little down at the moment.

SOPHIE: It's fine.

STEPHEN: Have you read any of Doris Rapp's books?

HILARY: No.

STEPHEN: How the corporate world is covering up the huge cancer increases caused by environmental pollution?

SOPHIE: I've read news items.

STEPHEN: Our bodies just aren't prepared for the new monster organic molecules those bastards are pouring out into the biosphere. There's absolutely no doubt that the soaring cancer rates can be sheeted straight back to corporate greed. And weak governments that can't or won't control them. But if your shares are doing very nicely thank you, then who cares if a kid dies at twenty-three? Until it happens to you. Then you'll care. I swear to you you'll care more than you ever thought possible. Don't worry, I won't say any of this when Jim and Dick get back. I just get the sense that with you two it's worth saying.

HILARY & SOPHIE: [*together*] It is.

STEPHEN: I especially appreciate it from you, Hilary. You must be really mad at me. All that money.

HILARY: If it was my son I'd be just as desperate.

STEPHEN: Jim turned out to be right, of course. The guy was a total fraud. But I truly appreciate what you and Dick did. More than you'll ever understand.

HILARY: It was Dick's decision.

STEPHEN: He said he asked you and you said it was okay, and now I've blown a hundred thousand.

SOPHIE: A hundred thousand?

STEPHEN: This American guy. Found him on the web. Claimed to have cured hundreds with focussed meditation and diet. Had dozens of testimonials up on his website and I phoned the people and the ones I spoke to swore by this guy. And said the expense was legitimate because the diet was supplemented by rare mushrooms and herbs. They really did swear by the guy. I realise now that there are always a percentage of people who go into temporary remission. Some of them for quite a while. But when you're as desperate as I was you *want* to believe. So desperately that you're easy prey for scum like that. I can't tell you how convincing he was. Deep southern drawl, grey hair, powder blue eyes and that practised look of utter caring on his face. Utter caring. And now the prick's got Dick's hundred thousand dollars and my son's dead. I wanted to shoot him. Could've got a gun. Poke your hand out with a hundred dollars in it in the US and you'll have a gun in it in ten minutes. I was on the edge. I was downright dangerous, but I finally told myself I had a bigger mission in life. To try and make sure that as many people as possible know that there was this great kid called Daniel who should've lived a lot longer than his father, but he didn't. And I've got another obligation. To pay back the money I owe to two of the most decent human beings on the face of this miserable, selfish, meaningless globe.

HILARY: Stephen, it's fine. We knew you had limited means and we made the decision knowing that. I'm more sorry than you can imagine that the guy was a fraud. To tell you the truth, when I read the material you sent us I kind of half believed him too. And I'm sure that if it had've been our son I would've believed totally.

STEPHEN: I'll be able to pay you back. Not all at once, but I will. That's what I'm here about.

HILARY: Stephen, if you can pay back some of it we'd appreciate it, but I don't want to make it the *raison d'être* of your life.

SOPHIE: Did you ask Jim for some help?

There's a silence. SOPHIE *realises what this means.*

He said no?

STEPHEN: He was right to. What I was asking was outrageous. I was just a little crazy at the time.

SOPHIE: Who wouldn't be, in your situation. He just said no?

STEPHEN: Jim knew the guy was a fake. I showed him all the stuff and he looked into it and told me to save my money. I should have listened.

SOPHIE: Yes, but—

STEPHEN: Jim was very straight and honest with me. He said he was very sorry about Daniel. And he was. But the money wasn't going to help. I hated him at the time, but I don't bear a grudge now because he was totally right.

HILARY: I have to say, Sophie, that given how upset Stephen was and given how much wealthier than us Jim is, I was pretty disgusted that he left it to Dick and me.

STEPHEN: No, really, he was right. His attitude was totally reasonable.

SOPHIE: Stephen, if he'd told me anything about it I would've insisted he helped.

STEPHEN: Please. I didn't come here to pay out Jim. He was absolutely right and part of the reason I'm here is to apologise to him for screaming at him.

SOPHIE: I don't wonder that you did. Jim can spend more than that on a five-day Caribbean cruise.

STEPHEN: No, please. He was perfectly right.

SOPHIE: Sorry. He was heartless. [*To* HILARY] He knew you two were paying?

HILARY: Certainly did. Dick rang him more than once to try and get him to contribute half.

STEPHEN: Look, that's all history, and the good news is I'll soon be in a position to start repayments. That's the reason I'm here.

HILARY: If you can, you can.

STEPHEN: [*to* SOPHIE] What a place you've got here. What a location. Sensational. You should see my place. A matchbox. Roof leaks, fibro walls, but hey, I can still look out and see something like that, and I can still step a few yards and walk on the beach. Last great thing about this country is they haven't yet privatised the beaches.

SOPHIE: They better not.

STEPHEN: It'll come. Like Europe, the US. If there's something beautiful, people want to own it and keep it for themselves.

SOPHIE: You're not wrong.

STEPHEN: Sorry, just can't stop talking. No one around at home but me, so I talk to myself, which they tell me is the first sign of madness. Biggest mistake I ever made was to call my boy Daniel. Now every time I hear 'Danny Boy' I'm a total mess. Did you know that it's about a father farewelling his son as he goes off to almost certain death?

SOPHIE: No.

STEPHEN: [*singing, surprisingly well*]
> 'The summer's gone, and all the flowers are dying,
> 'Tis you, 'tis you must go and I must bide.'

He looks at them with a trace of a tear in his eye.

Stupid name for any father to call his son. Oh, God. Tears. Sorry. Might go see the beach.

He starts to move off.

SOPHIE: I'll go too.

They head for the beach. STEPHEN *talks on as he goes.* HILARY *watches them.*

Natasha Elisabeth Beaumont as Sophie and Garry McDonald as Stephen in the 2004 Sydney Theatre Company production. (Photo: Tracey Schramm)

STEPHEN: Daniel hated the beach. Red hair, fair skin and a physique that wasn't exactly condoms stuffed with walnuts. His scene was more garages and electric guitars. Determined to be a rock star but was realistic enough to finally realise that if you can't sing or play guitar it ain't gonna be easy.

They exit. The lights go to black.

◆ ◆ ◆ ◆ ◆

SCENE TWO

The same place about an hour later.

JIM *and* DICK *enter.*

JIM: You would have nailed me if you hadn't gone to pieces on the last three holes.

DICK: [*shrugging*] Greg Norman's my role model.

JIM: Drink?

DICK: Light beer.

JIM: [*going to the fridge*] Same here. Pathetic how careful you get as the years roll by.

DICK: Realistic.

JIM: Remember Vera Caslavska, the Czech gymnast?

DICK: The Russians were just about to invade Czechoslovakia.

JIM: Had. Had invaded. She had to hide for three weeks just to get to Mexico. What a heroine.

DICK: I remember you telling us you were going to bed her. One of your few failures.

JIM: Too tiny. Given my endowment it would've been all just a bit too much.

He bursts out laughing. DICK *is less impressed.*

Remember that Peruvian stunner I was chasing until someone told me she was a pistol champion.

He hands DICK *a drink.*

Specialty was moving targets.

He laughs again. DICK *smiles.*

Remember Tommy Smith and John Carlos up on the victory dais, stars and stripes playing and they give the black power salute. [*He does it.*] Like 'Fuck you, America. What did you ever do for me?' I did it too. Had tears in my eyes. [*He gives the black power salute with fervour.*] Everyone started doing it. All over the Village. Remember how pathetic the drug tests were back then? Everyone was on everything they could swallow. Including us.

DICK: Except Stephen.

JIM: Moral, fucking Stephen. Arsehole. [*Imitating him*] 'I'm not taking anything that's going to fuck me up in the long term.' Only words he said the whole time we were there. Well, hello Stephen. It's long term and look who's fucked up. You, not us. If he'd done what everyone else was doing we would've had gold.

DICK: I think he still pulled his weight.

JIM: We would've won.

DICK: Come on. Those East Germans were light years ahead of us in the drugs thing. They were taking things we'd never even heard of.

JIM: State sponsored.

DICK: The only one who got caught was that poor Swede in the pentathlon.

JIM: [*laughing*] Tested positive for alcohol. From a party the night before.

He laughs loudly. This time DICK *joins in.*

Dick. Great days.

DICK: Yeah.

JIM: God, we were close, weren't we? The Amigos.

DICK: Too close in some ways.

JIM: That thing with Roger?

DICK: What the hell was I thinking?

JIM: It was the era. Try anything.

DICK: Yeah.

JIM: How did he actually—sort of—approach you?

DICK: I don't want to talk about it.

JIM: No really.

DICK: [*reluctantly*] He just came up to me in the shower one day and grabbed it.

JIM: Your dick?

> DICK *nods.*

Jesus.

DICK: He whispered in my ear, 'Stand still'. I was so startled I did. And ten seconds later…

JIM: What?

> DICK *throws his hands apart to indicate ejaculation.*

Jesus.

DICK: And he whispered, 'That's nothing. It gets much better.'

JIM: And did it?

DICK: I can't remember.

JIM: Oh, come on.

DICK: I can't.

JIM: You seemed to be enjoying it when we walked in on you.

DICK: Don't remind me.

JIM: You were.

DICK: All right. It was exciting, but I felt rotten after. It just wasn't my thing.

JIM: How come he came on to you?

DICK: What are you suggesting?

JIM: Nothing.

DICK: That I'm gay?

JIM: No.

DICK: I'm not.

JIM: Being attracted to you like that. It's just odd.

DICK: By that criterion you'd be well and truly gay.

JIM: What?

DICK: He told me the one he really wanted to fuck was you.

JIM: What?

DICK: He was obsessed by you.

JIM: If he'd tried that shower thing on me I'd've flattened him.

DICK: That's what he was scared of.

JIM: He was obsessed by me?

DICK: Absolutely.

JIM: That's bullshit.

DICK: Said you had the sexiest body he'd ever seen.

JIM: Bullshit.

DICK: Yes. He was obsessed.

JIM: That's sick.

DICK: Didn't you suspect?

JIM: No!

DICK: He was devastated when you didn't come and see him.

JIM: Well, I'm glad I didn't!

DICK: Would've made such a difference to him. I didn't tell him I'd called you three times to try and get you there.

JIM: All right. I'm sorry.

DICK: It was pretty callous. He still loved you in a weird way.

JIM: Don't say that!

DICK: Said you were a total bastard, but he still was crazy about you. Had your picture up by his bed.

JIM: No!

DICK: You just should know. If you think Roger being attracted to someone is a sign they're gay then you were the gayest of all.

JIM: You were the one he went for, because he knew I was straight!

DICK: So you're still saying I'm gay?

JIM: It's bloody odd he went for you.

DICK: Mate, you're looking at the straightest man in this room. By a country mile.

JIM: What's that mean?

DICK: If you'd spent what I've...

JIM: Spent what?

DICK: Doesn't matter.

JIM: Spent what? On women?

DICK: Doesn't matter.

JIM: You got a lover or something?

DICK: No.

JIM: Hookers?

DICK: Can we just leave this?

JIM: Hookers?

DICK: I'm gay? You kidding? Could've been a lot wealthier than I am if
    I was.

JIM: Hookers? You? You're kidding.

DICK: Will you keep it down?

JIM: Hookers?

DICK: No, not hookers. Top end of the market.

JIM: Brothel?

DICK: [*nodding*] 'Discrete Charm'.

JIM: [*whistling*] That *is* top of the market. God, you're a sly one, aren't
    you? Hilary know?

DICK: You kidding?

JIM: Are you still…?

DICK: No. Had to give it up years ago. Got too expensive. Too risky.
    Accountant started asking where all the money was going. And,
    frankly, the guilt was getting to me too. An attractive wife. What the
    hell was I doing?

Gary Day (left) as Jim and Tony Llewellyn-Jones as Dick in the
2004 Sydney Theatre Company production. (Photo: Tracey
Schramm)

JIM: Yes, I guess the trustees of that new hospital wing would ask themselves what the hell you were doing too.

DICK: Yeah.

JIM: I could never pay for sex.

DICK: That's your loss. Some of them were gorgeous.

JIM: How could you bear to make love to a woman who'd had hundreds of other men?

DICK: They make you feel you're the only one.

JIM: Dick, come on, they're sluts.

DICK: Not these ones.

JIM: They're sluts.

DICK: They were gorgeous.

JIM: Jesus, don't rhapsodise about prostitutes.

DICK: There was one—

JIM: Dick.

DICK: French. Blonde. Fantastic in bed.

JIM: Dick.

DICK: Anytime I hear French I get an erection.

JIM: Dick, you're sick.

DICK: You're just narrow minded.

JIM: Dick, I would never ever fuck a prostitute. Never have, never will.

DICK: You don't know what you've missed.

JIM: Hilary doesn't know?

DICK: Of course she doesn't.

> JIM *is silent.* DICK *looks at him with growing alarm.*

Jim, I just told you this to prove I wasn't gay.

JIM: I'm convinced.

DICK: Strictest confidence.

JIM: Absolutely.

DICK: Jim.

JIM: What?

DICK: Jim, no.

JIM: What?

DICK: I told you I'd try and swing it for you.

JIM: Of course you did. And I believe you.

DICK: But I can't guarantee anything.

JIM: I know.

DICK: There are a lot of other Council members.

JIM: Of course. You'll do your best. That's all I ask.

DICK: I will.

JIM: You don't seriously think I'd tell Hilary something like that just because I didn't get a few lousy letters after my name.

DICK: I'll be trying, but I can't guarantee.

JIM: I've got every confidence.

DICK: It just might be a little tricky.

JIM: Why?

DICK: Some of them have friends you've done business with.

JIM: Business is business.

DICK: Yeah.

JIM: I play it tough, but I break no laws.

DICK: Yeah.

JIM: So you've discussed this already? My application.

DICK: No!

JIM: I have to say I'm going to be pretty pissed if I don't get those letters, Dick. Especially knowing my oldest friend is in there hopefully rooting for me.

DICK: It'll be fine. I just can't guarantee. One of them's heard you tell that hawk story.

JIM: Dick. There's only one person I've ever told that story to.

DICK: You must've told it to others.

JIM: So you've already been hard at work blocking me, eh? You told the Domitian stuff. Life draining out of their eyes?

DICK: I said it as a joke. What a character you were.

JIM: Yeah, I'm sure.

DICK: I did.

JIM: When I'm dealing with a smug prick who thinks I'm fool enough to financially wet nurse them forever, then yes, I like watching the knife sink in. Because they deserve it. The world owes *no one* a living. I think, 'Buddy, here's a little shock for you. Learn what the real world's about.' [*He mimes plunging in the knife.*] Because they *deserve* it. Well, you're one hell of a friend, aren't you?

DICK: You're not liked out there, Jim. You're hugely successful, but you're not liked. Shoot the messenger, but it's true.

JIM: If you think I'm a such bastard, I'd better start acting like one.

DICK: Jim.

JIM: Let's do carrot and stick. Stick first. The right letters after my name or Hilary gets to hear.

DICK: You bastard!

JIM: Correct. Carrot. I've checked and your fund raising efforts for the new Richard McLean heart wing aren't going so well, are they?

DICK: We're doing fine.

JIM: You'll never be good at fund raising, Dick. The thing people hate most in the world is giving away cash. You can't apply the garrotte.

DICK: We'll get there.

JIM: Five million. And when this city hears the meanest bastard in town has given five they'll be queuing up out of shame.

DICK: Five million.

JIM: [*nodding*] Carrot was always part of the plan. Stick's been a bonus.

> DICK *is silent.*

I knew that whatever assurances you gave to my face, you'd be doing your best to torpedo me behind my back. And guess what? I was right.

DICK: It will look like you've bribed me.

JIM: You won't get it until well after the honours have been announced.

> DICK *is silent.*

If your fund makes its target you'll have a brand new hospital wing named after you. Much better than an A.C.

DICK: You know something, Jim? Of all the people that deserve to have those letters after their name, you're right near the bottom of the list.

JIM: The offer's there, Dick. Take it or leave it.

> DICK *looks away. The lights go to black.*

❖ ❖ ❖ ❖ ❖

SCENE THREE

The beach.

STEPHEN *and* SOPHIE *sit side by side on the beach.*

STEPHEN: When he was sixteen or so he just turned up on my doorstep. I hadn't seen him for two years. And he was angry about that and I didn't quite know what to do so we went to the movies. He'd shot up that year. Real beanpole. When we sat down this smart arse behind us says, 'Hey, Lanky, will you bloody well shift seats so me girlfriend can see?' Huge laugh from all his cronies. I sensed Daniel was very sensitive about his height so I went ballistic. I said, 'If anyone's going to shift, mate, it's going to be you, and if you've got a problem with that let's go outside and I'll beat the shit out of you'. Now I have to say this is highly unusual for me. I'm usually very much Clark Kent, not Superman. But at one level it's really a revelation to me—just how protective I am to the kid. How much I love him. But this doesn't occur to me until later because right at that moment I'm about to get beaten to death by this very large guy and three of his mates. Now Daniel's very ambivalent about his old man, but he doesn't want me to die, so he says, 'No problems, mate. We'll swap rows.' And he smiles at the girlfriend and says, 'If I'd paid good money for a movie I'd want to see it too'. And the guy says sheepishly, 'Sorry, mate. Didn't mean to offend.' So we swapped rows and in no time Daniel's talking to them about guitars and bands and Holden HRs. Unlike me, he was just so good with people. But the important thing is that when he saw me flare up like that he knew, for the first time he really knew, that I cared. And that was a real turning point. Sorry.

SOPHIE: [*putting her hand on his arm*] No. Please. I really want to hear.

STEPHEN: But he wasn't a wimp. When there was a point of principle— wow. Couldn't budge him.

SOPHIE *nods. The lights go to black.*

◆ ◆ ◆ ◆ ◆

SCENE FOUR

The living room.

JIM *is sitting reading the* Financial Times. DICK *enters.*

JIM: Computer okay?
DICK: Worked fine.
JIM: Collected your emails?
DICK: Collected a few. Sent a few.
JIM: Anything important?
DICK: Not really.

>SOPHIE *and* STEPHEN *enter.* JIM *looks up in surprise.*

JIM: Steve?
DICK: Steve?
STEPHEN: Heard you were both here, and I had to see you.
SOPHIE: Stephen's staying a few days.
JIM: [*unsettled*] Fine. Sure. [*To* STEPHEN] Like a drink?
STEPHEN: No, I'm fine.
JIM: Sorry about your son.
STEPHEN: Daniel.
JIM: Daniel.
STEPHEN: I'm sorry I screamed at you.
JIM: Stephen, I knew exactly where you were coming from and I understood.
STEPHEN: You were quite right. The guy was a total fraud.
JIM: Hey, Dick and I were just talking about Mexico '68. What an amazing time, eh?
STEPHEN: Amazing.

>JIM *does the black power salute.* STEPHEN *nods in recognition.*
>HILARY *comes in from the next room.*

JIM: We were all revolutionaries then, eh?
STEPHEN: Yeah.
JIM: Peace, love, the whole damn thing.
STEPHEN: Yeah.
JIM: The Grateful Dead, Jefferson Airplane, Mama Cass?

STEPHEN: Yeah.

JIM: I'm really sorry about… Daniel.

STEPHEN: You were absolutely right. The guy was a fraud.

JIM: I did some research.

STEPHEN: Of course.

JIM: If the money was really going to help then I would've been the first to write out the cheque.

STEPHEN: Yeah. Dick, Hilary. Sorry.

DICK: We were glad to help. Well, glad's perhaps an overstatement. Willing.

STEPHEN: Anything to get me off the phone?

HILARY: We could understand how you felt.

SOPHIE: I wish you'd told me about this, Jim.

JIM: It was between Stephen and me.

SOPHIE: Dick discussed it with Hilary.

JIM: Hilary knew Stephen. You didn't.

SOPHIE: You should've at least shared the cost with Dick and Hilary. Fifty thousand's nothing to you.

JIM: When money can achieve something, then I spend it.

SOPHIE: You could've for once in your life been generous.

STEPHEN: Hey, no, I was being totally unreasonable.

JIM: [*angrily to* SOPHIE] When it makes sense to be generous, I'm generous.

SOPHIE: Like when?

JIM: When it makes sense, I'm generous.

DICK: He is. He's just offered to donate five million to my heart wing appeal.

SOPHIE: Five million?

JIM: Dick, let's not talk about that now.

DICK: [*mischievously*] I was just backing you up.

SOPHIE: [*to* JIM] Getting an AC is worth that much?

DICK: Sophie, there's no connection at all. I pointed out to Jim that I couldn't accept unless I resigned from the Council, which I've just done. By email.

> JIM *stares at him.*

So there's no question of his offer being tainted. Is there, Jim?

JIM: You're not getting a cent!

DICK: I didn't really expect I ever would. Even if I'd gone in there and got your letters, the promised money would somehow never materialise.

JIM: It won't now.

> STEPHEN, *who is now sitting down, takes out a pad and starts taking surreptitious notes.*

DICK: You'd ring me up with a sad story that your accountants had sat on you and would I take maybe half a million? Which would shrink in due course to maybe a hundred thousand, and that would come with a demand that there be a huge plaque with your name on it in the foyer. I'm not as naïve as I used to be, Jim.

JIM: You've thrown away the carrot. Haven't you forgotten the stick?

DICK: If you're vicious enough to use it, go right ahead.

JIM: In my own time, Dick. In my own time.

SOPHIE: You'd offer five million for two bloody letters after your name and not give fifty thousand to your oldest friend who was desperate.

JIM: Are all of you crazy? Dick's hundred thousand went straight into the pocket of a total shyster.

STEPHEN: Jim's right.

JIM: Of course I'm fucking right!

SOPHIE: Jim, sometimes you do things that aren't totally rational because you know they're right.

DICK: I knew I was throwing the money away, but I also knew that Stephen didn't know that.

JIM: Stephen, Stephen. For Christ's sake, we rowed together thirty years ago. He was a weird recluse then, and he's even weirder now. He was never a fucking friend. He was just the fourth rower we needed to win gold. And he wasn't even good enough to do that. Can we stop all this sentimental bullshit!

DICK: You're a total arsehole, Jim.

JIM: Handing over the money was just part of your lifelong act, Dick. Saint Richard. Fixer of hearts. Doer of good deeds. Talker of sweet talk. Loved by all. Bullshit. Ego's every bit as big as mine.

SOPHIE: Except for one thing. He *has* left the world a better place than you ever will!

JIM: Oh yeah, he's a real saint.

DICK: Go ahead. You will sooner or later in any case. Anything to stop me getting my name up on the heart wing.

HILARY: What is this stick you're talking about?

DICK: Fire away, Jim.

JIM: You know something? I don't give a stuff any more about the letters. And I wish you all the very best in your fund raising efforts. Don't like your chances, but if you succeed in getting your name up in stone, good luck to you. I'll just keep making myself and my shareholders rich.

HILARY: [*to* DICK] What does he mean, stick?

DICK: Just some dirt he's got on me which I'm sure he'll use sooner or later.

HILARY: If it's what I think it is, I wouldn't think so.

> DICK *and* JIM *look at her.*

There's no way he'd want that out in the public arena.

SOPHIE: Hilary.

JIM: Wouldn't affect me.

HILARY: You're unusually broad minded then.

SOPHIE: Hilary.

JIM: Not sure how his Board of Trustees would react though.

HILARY: To what? Come on, Jim, if you've got something to say, say it.

JIM: You want to know? Fine. I wonder how his Trustees would view him spending so much money on prostitutes that his accountant orders him to stop.

> *There's a silence.*

You wanted to know, Hilary. You wanted to know.

HILARY: *I'm* just wondering…

SOPHIE: Hilary.

HILARY: … how impressed your investors are going to be when they know that most of that money Dick was spending was on your wife.

> *There's another silence as* JIM *stares at* SOPHIE. SOPHIE *shrugs.*

DICK: Sophie?

SOPHIE: [*in a breathy French accent*] Actually my professional name was Angelique.

She pushes her hair up and does a baby doll pout. DICK
recognises it straight away.

JIM: [*to* SOPHIE] You worked as a prostitute?

SOPHIE: A gentleman's escort. Thanks, Hilary.

HILARY: My pleasure.

JIM: Jesus, if this ever gets out this is going to be a disaster.

HILARY: Don't ever let it.

JIM: [*to* SOPHIE] You think I'm going to stay married to someone who
   prostituted herself to him?!

SOPHIE: I hope not.

JIM: Okay. Call in some bloodsucking, feminist, divorce lawyer and try
   and bleed me dry. But don't think you'll get anywhere when your
   background comes out in court.

SOPHIE: If you want to bring my background out, fine. I'm sure a lot of
   your business rivals will be delighted.

JIM: Blackmail all the way, right?

*From left: Gary Day as Jim, Natasha Elisabeth Beaumont as Sophie
and Wendy Hughes as Hilary in the 2004 Sydney Theatre Company
production. (Photo: Tracey Schramm)*

SOPHIE: Jim, I don't want your money. I've got plenty, thanks to Dick.

JIM: Why the hell did you do it?

SOPHIE: Because I was poor, Jim. Some people are.

JIM: And I suppose he was a real tiger between the sheets.

SOPHIE: Actually, yes.

HILARY: Lucky you.

SOPHIE: I'll give you some tips.

JIM: I want out. I absolutely want out.

SOPHIE: Thank God. How you treated Stephen was the last bloody straw.

STEPHEN: [*taking notes, to* SOPHIE] Did you spell that A-N- G-E-L-I-Q-U-E?

JIM: What the hell do you think you're doing?

STEPHEN: Checking the spelling.

JIM: Are you taking notes?

STEPHEN: Ah, yeah.

JIM: Why?

STEPHEN: I want to get it accurate.

JIM: Accurate?

STEPHEN: I'm a writer.

JIM: Writer? You haven't had anything published in twenty years.

STEPHEN: That's all about to change.

JIM: What are you on about?

> STEPHEN *holds up the manuscript he brought in with him.*

STEPHEN: It's only a work in progress, but I've been offered a twenty-thousand-dollar advance. I can start paying back that money I owe.

HILARY: You're writing a book about us? This?

STEPHEN: No, no. It's about Daniel and me. A father trying to come to grips with the imminent death of his child. It's about the awful irony of it taking something horrific like this to make us both realise just how much we loved and needed each other.

JIM: Where do we come in?

STEPHEN: Once I'd started I had to tell the whole story. How I'd come to you two for help.

JIM: How I gave nothing and he did?

STEPHEN: I'm not being in the least judgemental.

JIM: The rest of the world will be!

DICK: Why are you still taking notes now?

STEPHEN: It's a story that keeps evolving. Some time back it started to become a story about the Four Amigos as well, which my publisher loves. Says it makes it fragmented and postmodern. Frankly, I can't stop it all coming out. It's as if I'm not even writing this. I just sit there and watch the words pour out. Everything's coming out. Everything.

JIM: Everything?

STEPHEN: The drug taking, the sex. Dick and Roger.

DICK: No!

HILARY: Dick and Roger?

STEPHEN: The intrigues. How we all got together and decided we were going to dump Jim because he was the weak link.

JIM: I was the anchor. The linchpin.

STEPHEN: And how Roger pleaded with us not to do it because it would destroy you. And how that probably cost us gold. And how you never visited him when he was dying. All that sort of stuff.

JIM: For God's sake, not this stuff today?

STEPHEN: It's fantastic. All the dark secrets finally tumble out. It's cathartic. Greek.

JIM: Greek? It's going to fuck the lot of us!

DICK: Stephen, you can't write the stuff you heard today!

STEPHEN: People are amazingly tolerant.

DICK: Stephen, no one's going to name a hospital wing after someone who—

HILARY: You and Roger?

DICK: It was just a bit of harmless experimentation!

STEPHEN: Dick, everyone's sexuality is complex. There are thousands and thousands of men out there who are going to read this and breathe a sigh of relief.

HILARY: Stephen, our marriage is going to seem a total farce!

STEPHEN: Absolutely not. When I visited you five years ago I was knocked out by the warmth between you. You discuss politics, issues, make jokes, laugh with each other. That's in there too.

JIM: Stephen, there are some things you just can't do.

STEPHEN: Jim, I'm out of that straitjacket.

JIM: They're going to see me as a total bastard.

STEPHEN: They already do. This'll round you out.

JIM: You know what you're doing, don't you? Destroying us to give yourself the fifteen minutes of fame you've always craved, you miserable bloody loser. What other low animal bastard would exploit the death of his son like this?

STEPHEN: [*stepping up to him*] Yeah, I've always wanted to be a writer. And yeah, this has given me a chance. [*With sudden intense anger*] But if you're suggesting that what I went through with Daniel wasn't real for me or that I'll in any way cheapen it when I put it on the page, then I might just beat you to death on the fucking spot!

DICK: Write about Daniel, Stephen, but not about us.

HILARY: Stephen, I can understand your grief. And the depth of it. But it's not literature that's pouring out of your head, it's therapy.

JIM: Exactly. You're trying to elevate some perfectly normal, gormless kid into some kind of genius saint.

STEPHEN: [*grabbing him*] You saw him once in your life, arsehole. Don't you try and tell me what he was!

SOPHIE *puts herself between* STEPHEN *and* JIM.

SOPHIE: Stephen, don't do anything. He's not worth it.

JIM: You're defending the guy who's about to reveal to the world that you're a hooker?

SOPHIE: Stephen, calm down.

STEPHEN *moves away and takes out his notebook.*

STEPHEN: What did you call him, Jim? Just a normal, gormless kid. [*He notes it down.*] That'll look very caring in print.

JIM: Just get out of here!

STEPHEN: I'm going. I've got absolutely everything I need.

He leaves. They all stand silently looking at each other.

◆ ◆ ◆ ◆ ◆

SCENE FIVE

Stephen's fibro shack. Nine months later.

STEPHEN *is sitting in a deck chair listening to a band from the late sixties.* SOPHIE *enters carrying a book. He looks up in surprise and flicks off the sound.*

STEPHEN: How did you track me down?

SOPHIE: Asked around.

STEPHEN: Have a seat. Drink?

SOPHIE: No, I'm not staying. Just drove down to ask you to autograph your book. Which I think is marvellous.

STEPHEN: Thanks.

SOPHIE: Extraordinarily moving and not a trace of sentimentality.

STEPHEN: Thank you.

  He signs inside the cover.

SOPHIE: The reviews I've read have been great.

STEPHEN: [*nodding, pleased*] They've been pretty positive, haven't they?

SOPHIE: And thanks so much for not including all that stuff about us.

STEPHEN: I never was going to. I just wanted to get back at Jim.

SOPHIE: [*laughing*] All that note taking. He was certain it was all going to come out.

STEPHEN: Just having a bit of fun.

SOPHIE: He spent a fortune on libel lawyers and they told him there was nothing he could do.

STEPHEN: You're still with him?

SOPHIE: [*nodding*] He's changed.

STEPHEN: Really?

SOPHIE: He hasn't turned into a saint or anything, but he's trying.

STEPHEN: There was something about him I always liked. What you saw was very much what you got.

SOPHIE: That hasn't changed.

STEPHEN: There was a part of me that would've loved to be as ruthless as he is, but I was never game to try it.

SOPHIE: [*nodding*] The bad guys in movies are always more interesting.

STEPHEN: He forgave you for your past?

SOPHIE: I swore to him that Dick was a total dud in bed, and he was fine. It was him who was desperate for me to stay.

STEPHEN: So he should be.

SOPHIE: Which put me in a very good bargaining position.

STEPHEN: Yeah?

SOPHIE: That's the other thing I came to tell you. I made him give Dick the hundred thousand Dick gave you.

STEPHEN: That's a relief. I thought for ten seconds this book was going to make me able to pay him back, but the truth is that half the print run will probably be pulped.

SOPHIE: You're kidding. After those reviews?

STEPHEN: I guess not many people want to go through what I did.

SOPHIE: I also made him give Dick the five million he promised for the heart wing.

STEPHEN: Great!

> SOPHIE *nods excitedly at her achievement.*

SOPHIE: And I made him let me get pregnant.

> *She shows him her shape side-on.* STEPHEN *finds it hard to notice any bulge.*

Only four months. But I've seen him in there on ultrasound.

STEPHEN: I hope he takes after you.

SOPHIE: When he gave in on everything I thought he really *must* love me quite a lot. I guess that's something.

> STEPHEN *nods. The lights go to black.*

◆ ◆ ◆ ◆ ◆

SCENE SIX

A city bar. Some weeks later.

DICK *sits at the bar and looks up as* JIM *approaches.*

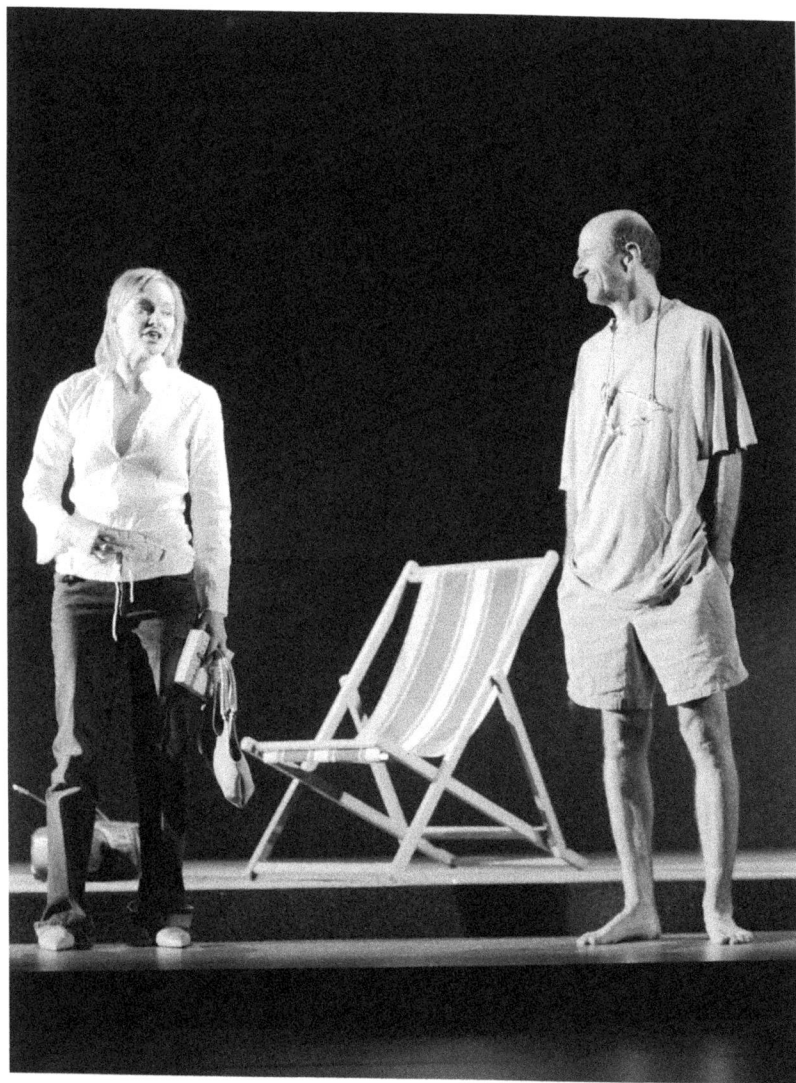

Natasha Elisabeth Beaumont as Sophie and Garry McDonald as Stephen in the 2004 Sydney Theatre Company production. (Photo: Tracey Schramm)

DICK: Congratulations!

> *They embrace like old buddies.*

   James Cartwright, AC.

JIM: It was donating the money to your bloody heart wing that did it.

DICK: Maybe.

JIM: For certain. Everybody knew you'd resigned from the Council, so for the first time in my life they couldn't pin an ulterior motive on me.

DICK: Pure philanthropy.

JIM: Bullshit. I was saving my marriage. How's yours?

DICK: I went through dark days, mate. Dark days. She walked out on me.

JIM: Yeah?

DICK: I was in a state of panic. I realised—that old cliché, but it's true—she really was my only close friend.

JIM: But she came back?

DICK: [*crossing his fingers*] Eventually. I had to give heaps to her bloody refugees, but she came back. And thank God. I realised I couldn't live without her. [*Pause.*] But don't count on ever getting together again as a foursome.

JIM: Women. Have to have 'em, but wish you didn't.

DICK: They say the same about us.

JIM: I hear you've reached target.

DICK: Last week, thanks to you.

JIM: You're getting your name up in stone?

DICK: Confirmed two days ago.

JIM: Hey!

> *They embrace again.*

   And that bloody loser Stephen. Book got a few good crits, but went straight down the tubes. Prick.

DICK: Never got himself out of the dropout mentality of the sixties.

JIM: You know that's absolutely right. Time-warp hippie.

DICK: Sophie… er… in good health?

JIM: Blooming. Happily giving away my money to any charity that'll have her on the board and needless to say they're lining up. I make it, she makes it disappear. But, hell, I can't live without her either.

DICK: Business booming.

JIM: Yeah, but I'm a bit worried I'm getting soft. This family guy, three kids, borrowed more than he should off us and I had him right over a barrel. I'm out on the golf course with him and I started to think, do I really want to see the life drain out of this guy's eyes. Eighteenth green, I look at him and say to myself, 'Yeah, bloody oath'. 'Sweetheart', I said, 'You're about to lose your business, but every setback is a challenge and every challenge is an opportunity'. And I loved it.

> DICK *stares at his friend. The lights go to black.*

◆ ◆ ◆ ◆ ◆

SCENE SEVEN

Stephen's beach shack. The same time.

STEPHEN *sits there in his deckchair at sunset. He gets up and talks softly to himself.*

STEPHEN: 'The summer's gone, and all the flowers are dying. 'Tis you, 'tis you must go and I must bide.'

> *Then walks a few steps towards the sound of the surf and stands there with the vast night sky as a backdrop.*

THE END

Also by David Williamson

After the Ball
Birthrights/ Soulmates
Brilliant Lies
The Club
Collected Plays Volume I
Collected Plays Volume II
Dead White Males
The Department
Don's Party
Emerald City
Flatfoot
The Great Man / Sanctuary
The Jack Manning Trilogy (Face to Face, A Conversation, Charitable
    Intent)
Money and Friends
The Perfectionist
The Removalists
Siren
Sons of Cain
Third World Blues
Top Silk
Up for Grabs / Corporate Vibes

About David Williamson

Brian Kiernan, *David Williamson: A Writer's Career*
David Moore, *David Williamson's Jack Manning Trilogy: A Study
    Guide*

After the Ball

Stephen has, with ill grace, returned home to his mother's deathbed. As he and his sister rake through the family photographs and childhood memories, they find conflicting versions of their parents' unhappy marriage.

2 Acts—3M, 6W

0 86819 537 5

Birthrights / Soulmates

Birthrights is a bittersweet play about motherhood. At 29, Helen has a vital operation that stops her from having what she desperately wants: a child. Her younger sister Claudia gives her a wonderful gift: she bears a child for her sister. However years later when Claudia finds out that she and her husband Martin can't conceive, she realises that the only baby she will ever bear is Kelly, the child she had for her sister.

Soulmates is about the slippery business of books and writing, commerce versus art, serious writing versus popular writing. Set in both Melbourne and New York, it is a tale of revenge as the best-selling expatriate author Katie Best engineers a scheme to bring her most craven critic Danny O'Loughlin undone.

2 Acts—2M, 4W; 2 Acts—4M, 3W

0 86819 698 3

Brilliant Lies

Williamson turns his penetrating eye and sharply focused wit to issues of 'political correctness' and sexual harassment. A serious comedy, *Brilliant Lies* is a stimulating contribution to the continuing debate on our changing social values.

2 Acts—4M, 3W

0 86819 371 2

The Club

Williamson's famous play about the uses and abuses of managerial power, which in 1976 predicted the destruction of Australian football, has proven even more prescient since the rise and fall of Super League.

2 Acts—6M

0 86819 013 6

Collected Plays: Volume 1

Williamson's vintage early plays: *The Coming of Stork; The Removalists; Don's Party; Jugglers Three;* and *What If You Died Tomorrow?.*

1 Act—5M, 1W; 2 Acts—4M, 2W; 2 Acts—6M, 5W; 1 Act—5M, 2W; 2 Acts—5M, 3W

0 86819 110 8

Collected Plays: Volume II

More plays from Australia's most popular playwright. This collection contains *A Handful of Friends; The Club; The Department;* and *Travelling North.*

2 Acts—2M, 3W; 2 Acts—6M; 2 Acts—8M, 2W; 2 Acts—3M, 4W

0 86819 287 2

Dead White Males

Postmodernism versus liberal humanism—can an older male academic convert a young female student to a post-structural, post-patriarchal view of literature and seduce her at the same time?

2 Acts—6W, 5M

0 86819 443 3

The Department

A staff meeting of the Engineering Department in a College of Advanced Education is the occasion in this play for an acute dissection of the workings of bureaucracy and the absurd politicking needed to support it.

2 Acts—8M, 2W

0 86819 022 5

Don's Party

On election night 1969, Don and Kath give a party to watch the results. As the tide turns against Labor, the good cheer palls, and the faded ideals and disappointed hopes of the characters begin to show.

2 Acts—6M, 5W

0 86819 530 8

Emerald City

Colin, a screenwriter, and his wife Kate, a publisher, move to the 'Emerald City' where fame and fortune are there for the taking, but surprises are in store for them both.

2 Acts—3M, 3W

0 86819 170 1

Flatfoot

Roman playwright Titus Maccius Plautus pops up in the 21st century, enraged to find his ideas have been plundered through the ages. To prove his point he takes us back to Ancient Rome, where he must convince his producer that his new play will be a hit. The trouble is the play hasn't been written, so Plautus must act it out before the cynical producer, making it up as he goes along.

2 Acts—2M, 1W

0 86819 735 1

The Great Man/Sanctuary

In *The Great Man,* a volatile group gathers to plan the funeral of a Labor Party icon. They all claim to know the truth about him, but their recollections are coloured by their own interests.

In a revised version of *Sanctuary,* a investigative journalist returns to Australia to retire, but a student working on his biography intervenes.
1 Act—4M, 3W; 2 Acts—2M
0 86819 633 9

The Jack Manning Trilogy
Here Australia's most popular playwright explores community conferenc-ing—a process bringing together the victims and perpetrators of a crime to attempt some kind of reconciliation. In *Face to Face*, when Glen comes face to face with the employee who rammed his Mercedes, he must acknowledge responsibility for a series of incidents which helped provoke the crime.

In *A Conversation,* the family of a rapist and murderer are confronted by the family of his victim.

Charitable Intent focuses on the pressures and contradictions that erupt as workplace values change.
1 Act—4M, 4W; 1 Act—6M, 4W; 1 Act—2M, 6W
0 86819 657 6

Money and Friends
Peter, a mathematician who is niceness itself, is in financial trouble because of his brother's bankruptcy. His neighbour Margaret decides he needs help from his friends who spend most of their lives boasting about their wealth.
2 Acts—5M, 4W
0 86819 314 3

The Perfectionist
Williamson's continuing examination of modern marriage follows a pair of academics from Denmark to Sydney as they blunder along the rival paths of career and parenthood. Introduced by Rodney Fisher.
2 Acts—3M, 2W
0 86819 069 1

The Removalists
A young policeman's first day on duty becomes a violent initiation into law enforcement. Remarkable for its blend of boisterous humour and horrifying violence, the play has built a classic reputation as a statement on authoritarianism.
2 Acts—4M, 2W
0 86819 038 1

Siren
Holed up in a Central Coast motel room with three undercover detectives, Liz has been employed to use her sex appeal on Billy Nottle, a local councillor suspected of accepting bribes from developers.
2 Acts—5M, 2W
0 86819 282 1

Sons of Cain

Against a background of disintegrating marital relationships and emotional greed, a newspaper editor with three investigative journalists takes on the Mr Bigs of the drug trade. The villain proves to be the nature of society itself.

2 Acts—6M, 3W

0 86819 179 5

Third World Blues

Williamson has revisited his early play *Jugglers Three,* first performed in 1972 (and published in Williamson's *Collected Plays Volume I*). The result is taut and dramatic, with the energy and biting satire of plays like *The Removalists* and *Don's Party.*

2 Acts—5M, 2W

0 86819 520 0

Travelling North

A moving homage to old age and the old radicals who changed the course of our history. Soon after Frank and Frances desert their former lives for a northerly bohemian retreat, Frank's mortality asserts itself.

2 Acts—3M, 4W

0 86819 270 8

Up For Grabs / Corporate Vibes

Art dealers: parasites or prophets? Simone Allen likes to see herself as the latter, but when given the opportunity to sell one of the better Whiteleys, her behaviour becomes less than angelic as the pressure mounts. Driven by greed and aesthetics, Williamson's characters discover how far they will go when more than just a beautiful work of art is *Up for Grabs* in this sexy comedy of manners.

In *Corporate Vibes,* a real estate developer faces a staff mutiny. When a man who is accustomed to getting his own way finds himself confronted by a softly-spoken mediator and a demand for buildings which 'delight the eye', the stage is set for a vintage farce.

2 Acts—3M, 4W; 2 Acts—3M, 4W

0 86819 653 3

For a full list of our titles, visit our website:

www.currency.com.au

Currency Press
The performing arts publisher
PO Box 2287
Strawberry Hills NSW 2012
Australia
enquiries@currency.com.au
Tel: (02) 9319 5877
Fax: (02) 9319 3649

www.ingramcontent.com/pod-product-compliance
Lightning Source LLC
Chambersburg PA
CBHW041932090426
42744CB00017B/2021